WASTE TO ENERGY IN THE AGE OF THE CIRCULAR ECONOMY

COMPENDIUM OF CASE STUDIES AND EMERGING TECHNOLOGIES

NOVEMBER 2020

ASIAN DEVELOPMENT BANK

CONTENTS

TABLES AND FIGURES

ABBREVIATIONS AND UNITS AND MEASURES

ADB	–	Asian Development Bank
BOOT	–	build–own–operate–transfer
CAPEX	–	capital expenditure
CBE	–	Clean Energy Community
CBG	–	compressed biomethane gas
CHP	–	combined heat and power
CIGAR	–	Covered-in-Ground Anaerobic Reactor
CNG	–	compressed natural gas
CNIM	–	Constructions Industrielles de la Méditerranée
COD	–	chemical oxygen demand
EFT	–	EcoFuel Technologies, Inc.
EPR	–	extended producer responsibility
GHG	–	greenhouse gas
HDPE	–	high-density polyethylene
HFO	–	heavy fuel oil
IDG	–	ID Gasifiers Pty, Ltd.
KPP	–	Kokonut Pacific Pty
KPSI	–	Kokonut Pacific Solomon Islands
LPG	–	liquified petroleum gas
LSFO	–	low sulfur fuel oil
MRF	–	material recovery facility
MSW	–	municipal solid waste
PAH	–	polycyclic aromatic hydrocarbon
PCPPI	–	Pepsi Cola Products Philippines, Inc.
PEA	–	Provincial Electricity Authority (Thailand)
PEM	–	plasma enhanced melter
PPA	–	power purchase agreement
PRC	–	People's Republic of China
PTF	–	plastics to fuel
RDF	–	refuse-derived fuel

SRF	–	solid recovered fuel
SZW	–	Saahas Zero Waste
TRL	–	technology readiness level
UK	–	United Kingdom
US	–	United States
WtE	–	waste to energy
ZWP	–	zero waste program

Units and Measures

GW	–	gigawatt
kCal	–	kilocalorie
kg	–	kilogram
kJ	–	kilojoule
kV	–	kilovolt
kW	–	kilowatt
kWe	–	kilowatt electrical
kWh	–	kilowatt-hour
m^3	–	cubic meter
MJ	–	megajoules
Mt	–	metric ton
MW	–	megawatt
MWe	–	megawatt electrical
MWh	–	megawatt-hour
MWt	–	megawatt thermal
Nm^3	–	normal cubic meter
T	–	tonne*
TPD	–	tons per day
tph	–	tons per hour
wt%	–	weight percent

---

*   T is referred to as tonne (metric) which is equivalent to 1,000 kilograms. In the US, ton is used, which is equivalent to 0.907185 tonne or 907.185 kilograms.

$1:€:0.756 as of 31 December 2012 (Source: https://forex.adb.org/fx_rate/getRates)

EXECUTIVE SUMMARY

This compendium to the *Waste to Energy in the Age of the Circular Economy Handbook* outlines waste-to-energy project implementations with background, technology, financing, operations, and lessons learned.

These projects start with a large municipal solid waste plant reducing unsorted waste, and progress through smaller distributed solutions that reduce components of the waste or process the waste to capture the energy contained.

Distributed business models to recycle and upcycle waste components using intermediate fuel technologies—including refuse derived fuels, biogas, biomethane, and syngas—are presented. The use of distributed gasification and pyrolysis is also demonstrated at the distributed scale. These upcycling activities reduce the required capacity for end-of-life facilities.

Models from India and the People's Republic of China are presented, showing smaller communities removing the need for end-of-life facilities.

A range of developing technologies in commercialization are presented in the second section. Readers should be aware of the technology readiness levels of a particular technology. The technology readiness level should be considered when committing to a particular technology.

The current linear (make, use, dispose) model is untenable with cities literally drowning in garbage. The opportunity to create jobs, energy, and resources are immense. A circular economy requires extensive redesign of everyday products—how they are delivered to the community, and how they can be incorporated into daily life. We need to progress firmly into a much stronger recycling economy. The type and capacity of waste-to-energy facilities will change as we progress through the recycling economy into a circular economy where nothing is wasted.

Determining the speed of that transition is a challenge for policy makers and planners around the world.

1 OVERVIEW OF WASTE-TO-ENERGY CASE STUDIES

Waste-to-energy (WtE) technologies and pathways are significant components of a circular economy. WtE technologies can be an effective means of recovering energy from residual wastes and reducing the volume of materials that go to the landfill. As of December 2018, there are more than 2,450 WtE plants that are operational worldwide with a total waste input capacity of around 368 million tons per year. It was estimated that more than 2,700 plants will be on-site by 2028.[1]

This section provides few examples of projects that are located in 12 countries using different WtE technologies. Most of the projects are within the Asia and Pacific region, but there are also few examples in Europe and Latin America. There is a wide variation on the size of the projects with initial costs ranging from a few thousand to hundreds of millions of dollars. Some initiatives are on pilot-scale while others are large investment projects that are invested in by private sector companies. Several business models are employed covering almost all types of WtE technologies such as thermal, thermal-mechanical, thermal-chemical, and bio-chemical. While anaerobic digestion (bio-chemical) is the most common technology among the featured projects, the biogas output also has a wide variety of applications. Biogas can be used as a source for power, combined heat and power, biomethane—a vehicle fuel, compressed biomethane, and fertilizer.

The featured projects followed a uniform format: context, solutions, technology, business model, financing structure, results, and lessons. A brief introduction of the project developer or technology provider is included as well as the key words and recommended further reading in case more information is required. On the first page, a summary is presented for each of the projects to highlight brief snapshot of the project's main features.

The project summaries were provided by invited organizations. The figures and images were provided by project developers. The Asian Development Bank (ADB) has made every effort to check information provided but is unable to verify exact information. In general, the project summaries represent a reasonable example of the specific technologies discussed. Some information could not be provided as they were subject to confidentiality and commercial confidence.

Readers should be mindful that additional research and assessment is required to ensure projects meet local laws and regulations. Specifically, gaseous and liquid emissions should be verified by credible third-party agencies. Additionally, the social impacts of any project need to be considered.

Table 1 presents the summary of the all the projects included in this section. These technologies are project- and developer-specific. These examples will give the reader a better idea of what has been done by the industry.

---

[1] Ecoprog GmbH. 2019. *Waste to Energy 2019/2020: Technologies, Plants, Projects, Players and Backgrounds of the Global Thermal Waste Treatment Business*. Extract. 12th ed. Cologne. https://www.ecoprog.com/fileadmin/user_upload/extract_market_report_WtE_2019-2020_ecoprog.pdf.

Table 1: Summary of Project Examples

#	Project Name	Capital ($ million)	Developer	Host	Country	Business Model	Technology	End use	Feedstock	Completion Year	Current Status	Pathway
1.	Baku Waste-to-Energy Plant	457.6	CNIM Group	Ministry of Economy of Azerbaijan Republic	Azerbaijan	Sales of electricity, collection and treatment tariffs, government subsidies	Direct Combustion	Power	MSW	2012	Active	1, 2
2.	Pilot Project Waste-to-Energy with Bio-Drying	0.3	Indocement	Indocement	Indonesia	Potential cost reduction of MSW compared to coal	Microbiological treatment	Fuel	MSW	2012	Not active since May 2017	4, 5, 10
3.	Decentralized Plastic Pyrolysis	0.0043	Caring Nature	Jeypee Farm	India	Sales of product	Pyrolysis	Transport fuel, fertilizer	Vegetable waste, plastics	2018	Active	5
4.	Plastic-to-Liquid Fuel	0.6	ScandGreen Energy	Quantafuel MX	Mexico	Pilot only	Pyrolysis	Diesel	Plastics	2017	Not active	5
5.	Ankur's Waste-to-Energy Project	0.3	Ankur Scientific Energy Technologies	Ankur Scientific Energy Technologies	India	Pilot plant	Gasification	Power	MSW	2017	Active	5
6.	HighCrest Corporation	3.4	IES Biogas	Broiler Farm	Philippines	Sales of electricity and fertilizer	Anaerobic digestion	Power	Chicken manure	2020	Unclear	5
7.	Decentralized Waste Management Model	0.08	Saahas Zero Waste	Saahas Zero Waste	India	Revenues from waste and service fee	Anaerobic digestion, mechanical-biological	Cooking	MSW	2020	Active	5,6,8,9
8.	Carbon Masters Koramangala plant	0.47	Carbon Masters India Pvt. Ltd	Carbon Masters India Pvt. Ltd	India	Sales of bio-CNG and fertilizer	Anaerobic digestion	Fertilizer, compressed gas	Organic waste	2018	Active	5
9.	Combined Heat and Power facility	5.8	SUREPEP Inc.	Pepsi Cola Products Philippines Inc	Philippines	Direct contract with Pepsi Cola (10 years)	Direct combustion	Steam and power	Rice husk	2015	Active (steam only)	5
10.	150-kWe Power Generation in Dual Fuel Mode	.045	Ankur Scientific Energy Technologies	MS Rice Industries	India	Electricity reliability and reduced cost to diesel power generation	Gasification	Power	Rice husk	2015	Active	5

#	Project Name	Capital ($ million)	Developer	Host	Country	Business Model	Technology	End use	Feedstock	Completion Year	Current Status	Pathway
11.	Australian Bio Fert Small-Scale Biological Fertilizer Demonstration and Product	3.5	ideas*/Torreco	Australia Bio Fert Pty Ltd	Australia	Waste management fees and sales of products	Torrefaction	Fertilizer	Chicken manure, litter, and dead bird	2019	Not active	5, 10
12.	CBE—Clean Energy Community	11.0	SBANG Sustainable Energies	SBANG Sustainable Energies	Thailand	Sale of electricity via 20 years power purchase agreement	Direct Combustion	Power	Multi-fuel: agricultural residues	2018	Active	1
13.	ID Gasifiers Coconut shell-Fueled Module—Coconut Technology Centre Development	0.014	ID Gasifiers Pty Ltd	Kokonut Pacific Pty Ltd	Solomon Islands	Pilot trial	Gasification	Power, heat, biochar	Coconut shell	2016	Unclear	5
14.	Sumilao Farm Waste-to-Energy	4.7	Solutions Using Renewable Energy (SURE) Eco Energy Philippines Inc	San Miguel Purefoods, Inc	Philippines	Direct contract with SMFI (8 years)	Anaerobic digestion	Power	Animal waste	2016	Active	5
15.	WtE Siang Phong Biogas	3.3	HD&L Co. Ltd	Siang Phong Development Agriculture Co. Ltd	Cambodia	Cost savings compared to using heavy fuel oil	Anaerobic digestion	CHP	Cassava root cake and root wash	2012	Active	5
16.	Kitroongruang Compressed Biomethane Gas (KIT-CBG) Project	1.0	Asia Biogas	KRR Starch	Thailand	Sales of product	Anaerobic digestion	Transport fuel, fertilizer	Cassava pulp	2018	Active	5, 10
17.	Rainbarrow Farm Poundbury	1.54	DMT Environmental Technology	JV Energen	United Kingdom	Sales of gas via direct injection to the grid	Anaerobic digestion	CHP	Maize, grass, potato waste, whey food waste	2012	Active	5
18.	Yitong Distributed Waste-to-Energy Project	7.0	Yitong Co. Ltd	Yitong Co. Ltd	People's Republic of China	Sales of heating, power, and fertilizer	Anaerobic digestion	Heat, fertilizer	Animal feces, human feces, rice straw	2018	Active	3,4,5,7,9, 10

CHP = combined heat and power, CNG = compressed natural gas, kWe = kilowatt electrical, MSW = municipal solid waste, WtE = waste-to-energy.
Source: Stephen Peters, ADB.

1.1 Baku Waste-to-Energy Plant

CONTEXT

The history of Baku Waste-to-Energy (WtE) Project is largely associated with Balakhani waste landfill, which was constructed in 1963. The Balakhani landfill handles about 3.8 million to 4.0 million cubic meters (m^3) of solid waste per annum. According to an environmental and social impact assessment report by the World Bank, 90% of total waste generated in Baku City was disposed in Balakhani landfill.

Balakhani is the major waste landfill where all city refuse in Greater Baku are dumped. Balakhani landfill was managed without regard for environmental implications, and has caused pollution of the nearby Boyuk Shor Lake. It also posed damage to the neighboring areas, including residential areas due to foul odor caused by the garbage. Landfill open fires also caused air pollution.

Many similar landfills appeared outside the city center. The same situation occurred in newly established residential zones and in areas where the communal services are inadequate.

The Balakhani landfill as well as other informal landfills created serious health hazards to the population. According to international experts, proper and systematic management of solid waste collection, transportation, sorting, and processing are essential to improve the environmental conditions in the area.

The Baku WtE project was implemented in 2006 as part of the series of measures taken by the Government of Azerbaijan to protect the environment. The Ministry of Economy provided project oversight. The state-owned company Tamiz Shahar JSC, which is responsible for the utilization of the solid municipal waste in Baku City, awarded in December 2008 a 20-year contract to Constructions Industrielles de la Méditerranée (CNIM) for the design, construction, and operation of an energy recovery facility. This flagship project covering 10 hectares of land is one of the largest facilities built in Europe. The construction of Baku WtE Plant began in 2009 and was completed in 2012. Figure 1 shows the location of the Baku waste-to-energy project.

<table>
<tr><td colspan="2">PROJECT SUMMARY</td></tr>
<tr><td colspan="2">PROJECT NAME:
Baku Waste-to-Energy Plant</td></tr>
<tr><td colspan="2">CAPITAL COST:
$457.6 million (€346 million)[2]</td></tr>
<tr><td colspan="2">DEVELOPER:
CNIM Group</td></tr>
<tr><td colspan="2">PROJECT HOST:
Ministry of Economy of the Republic of Azerbaijan</td></tr>
<tr><td colspan="2">GEOGRAPHICAL LOCATION:
Balakhani Settlement, Baku, Azerbaijan</td></tr>
<tr><td colspan="2">TYPE OF ENERGY PROJECT:
Waste Valorization to Electrical Power</td></tr>
<tr><td colspan="2">PROJECT COMPLETION YEAR:
2012</td></tr>
</table>

---

[2] $1:€:0.756 as of 31 December 2012 (Source: https://forex.adb.org/fx_rate/getRates).

Figure 1: Location of the Baku Waste-to-Energy Project

Source: Constructions Industrielles de la Méditerranée (CNIM) Group.

SOLUTION

CNIM designed and built the Baku WtE Plant on a turnkey basis. It is now being operated by CNIM Azerbaijan, Ltd., a subsidiary of CNIM Group, for a period of 20 years. The construction of the plant took 4 years and became fully operational in December 2012.

Designed to meet the strict environmental standards, the plant complies with the most stringent European regulations, in particular, emission standards, thanks to the flue gas treatment system designed by CNIM subsidiary, Lab. The project reemphasized CNIM's commitment in protecting the environment, human health, and climate through the displacement of fossil fuels.

The facility, which took its architectural inspiration from Azerbaijan *mashrabiyas,* is the 150th plant built by CNIM (Figure 2). Consisting of two waste combustion units with a capacity of 33 tons per hour each, the plant can treat 500,000 tons of household waste and 10,000 tons of hospital waste per annum. The 231,500 megawatt-hour (MWh) of electricity generated by the WtE plant can supply electricity to more than 50,000 households. Flue gas is treated by a semi-dry process in conjunction with a non-catalytic deNOx process. Bottom ashes are treated to recover and recycle ferrous metals. They are stored for possible use for road construction of the mineral fraction.

Baku Waste-to-Energy Plant. This facility in Azerbaijan can treat 500,000 tons of household waste and 10,000 tons of hospital waste per annum (photo by Tamiz Shahar).

TECHNOLOGY

The Baku WtE Plant is composed of two production lines with combustion capacity of 33 tons per hour per line at a nominal calorific value of 8,500 kilojoules (kJ)/kilogram (kg). Below are the four main process flows (Figure 3).

(i)   Municipal solid waste is tipped into the storage bunker (1) by refuse collection trucks. Sorting of recyclable part of domestic waste is realized off-site.

(ii)   Transfer of residual municipal waste (A) via overhead cranes from bunker to the hopper (2). It passes down the chute to the combustion chamber and the reverse-acting grate via hydraulic feeders (3). The ashes (H) are separated in the slag separator system.

(iii) In the furnace, the energy available in waste is released as hot flue gases. The combustion heat is recovered with the multi-pass steam-water boiler located above the furnace (5). High-temperature steam is generated and fed to the turbo generator with high-energy efficiency.

(iv)   The high temperatures obtained in the combustion chamber destroy any odors and bio-pollutants. Flue gases are completely cleaned before the stack in order to remove all micro-pollutants (dust and chemicals) coming from the waste (6 and 7).

(v)   The superheated steam leaving the boiler is fed directly to a turbo generator, which turns its energy into electricity (9 and 10). At the exhaust from the turbine, the steam is cooled down and condensed in an air-cooled condenser (11). The condensate water returns to the boilers' drums for subsequent injection to this water–steam closed loop (12 and 13).

During this process, 37 megawatts (MW) of electric energy is generated, of which 5 MW is intended for plant own use and the other 32 MW is to be supplied to the local electric network via 11 kilovolts (kV)/110 kV step-up transformers.

The waste collection principle has been designed with consideration to the uneven and complex characteristics of the municipal waste, especially in the cities where wastes are not properly segregated at source. The tipping hall allows pretreatment and removal of pieces of materials unsuitable for burning or when shredding is required. The waste bunker is sufficient to collect waste for 7 consecutive days and has the capacity of storing 15,000 m^3 of waste. The overhead moving crane transfers the waste from the bunker to combustion furnaces. Combustion takes place on a CNIM/Martin GmbH grate with infrared pyrometer combustion control. This reverse-acting grate is the number one and state-of-the-art process in the world for municipal solid waste (MSW) combustion. This technology has demonstrated its performances and flexibility for a complete combustion of highly variable and heterogeneous fuel. It avoids the emissions of toxic gases such as carbon monoxide (CO). The grate deals with all types of municipal waste without the need for pretreatment or grate water cooling.

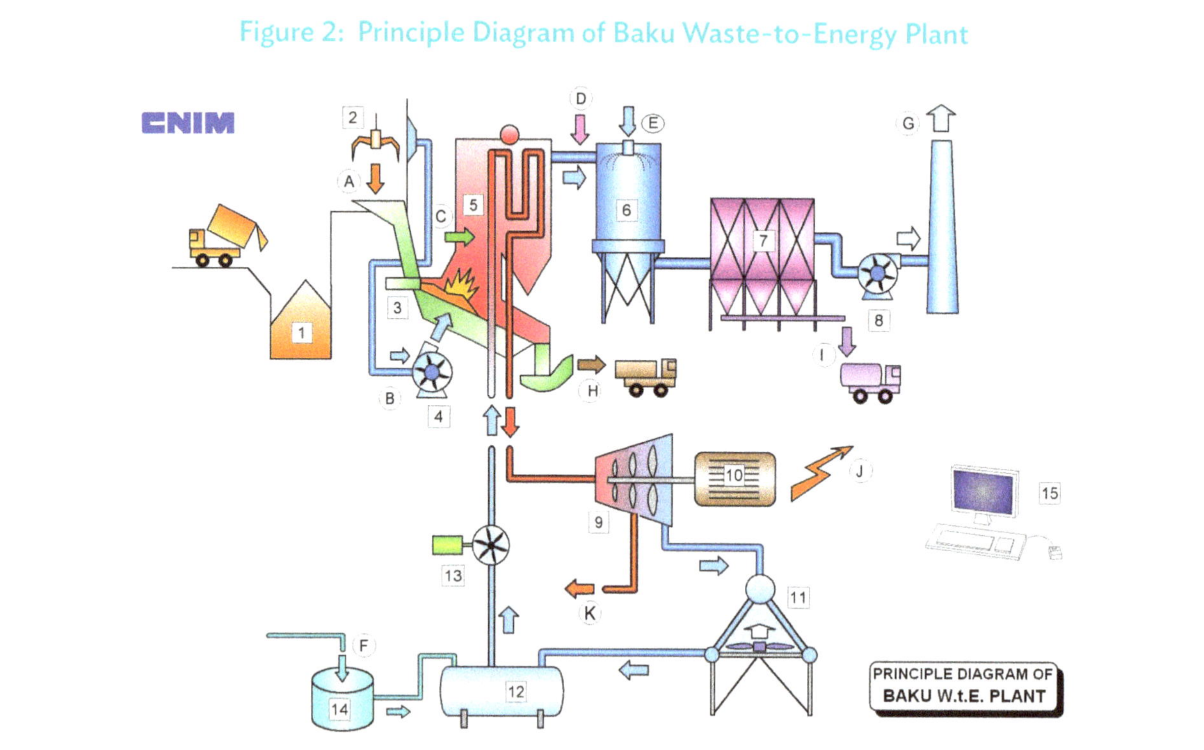

Figure 2: Principle Diagram of Baku Waste-to-Energy Plant

Legend: EQUIPMENT: 1- Waste bunker, 2- Traveling crane and grab, 3- CNIM/MARTIN GmbH combustion grate, 4- Combustion air supply, 5- CNIM recovery boiler, 6- LAB Semi-dry type reactor, 7- Fabric filter, 8- Induced draft fan, 9- Steam turbine, 10-Alternator, 11-Air cooled condenser, 12-Deaerator and feed water tank, 13- Feed water pumps, 14- Feed water treatment and demineralized water tank, 15-Operation and control unit in control room.

INPUT: A- Waste; B- Air, C- Urea solution, D- Activated carbon, E- Lime slurry, F- Raw water.

OUTPUT: G-Clean flue gas, H- Coarse ash (clinker) to storage and maturation area, I- Fly ash and flue gas treatment by-products, J- Electricity, K- Steam to district heating network (future possibility).

Source: Constructions Industrielles de la Méditerranée (CNIM) Group.

The heat produced by combustion and carried in the flue gases is recovered in a CNIM recovery steam boiler installed above the grate. This produces superheated steam at high pressure and temperature that are regulated. The produced steam is used on a steam turbine connected to a power generator unit. At the exhaust from the turbine, the steam is cooled down and condensed in an air-cooled condenser. The condensate water returns to the boilers' drums for subsequent injection to this water–steam closed loop.

At the outlet of the boiler, the hot flue gases are treated in a LAB group CNIM semi-dry process, which is based first on a spray dryer reactor and then a bag house filter. Consumables are limited to quick lime to neutralize the acid gases and activated carbon to separate volatile heavy metals and toxic organic compounds. The control loop for lime slurry injection uses the measurements of upstream and downstream hydrogen chloride (HCl) and sulfur oxides (SOx) values to optimize quick lime consumption and solid residue production.

Before releasing to the atmosphere, the physical properties (temperature, pressure, and flow rate) and pollutants contents of the flue gas (SO_2, HCl, NOx, NH3, CO, TOC, dust) as well as O_2, CO_2 and H_2O are continuously measured by the gas analyzers. Analyzer signals are transmitted to the data recording system and monitored 24/7 from the control room. The WtE plant is designed to operate year-round, 24/7. The expected lifetime of the plant is at least 35 years.

The aim of this project was to improve the environment of Baku. Focus was made to lower the environmental and health impact of the power plant as well as conserve natural resources during plant operation. Reduction on water utilization was made possible by installing closed loop water systems and maximizing rainwater harvesting through distinct roof structure design and comprehensive drainage system. Figure 4 illustrates the water collection system and the discharge process.

These supplied technologies are part of the Best Available Techniques (BAT) which are described by the BAT Reference document published by the European Commission.

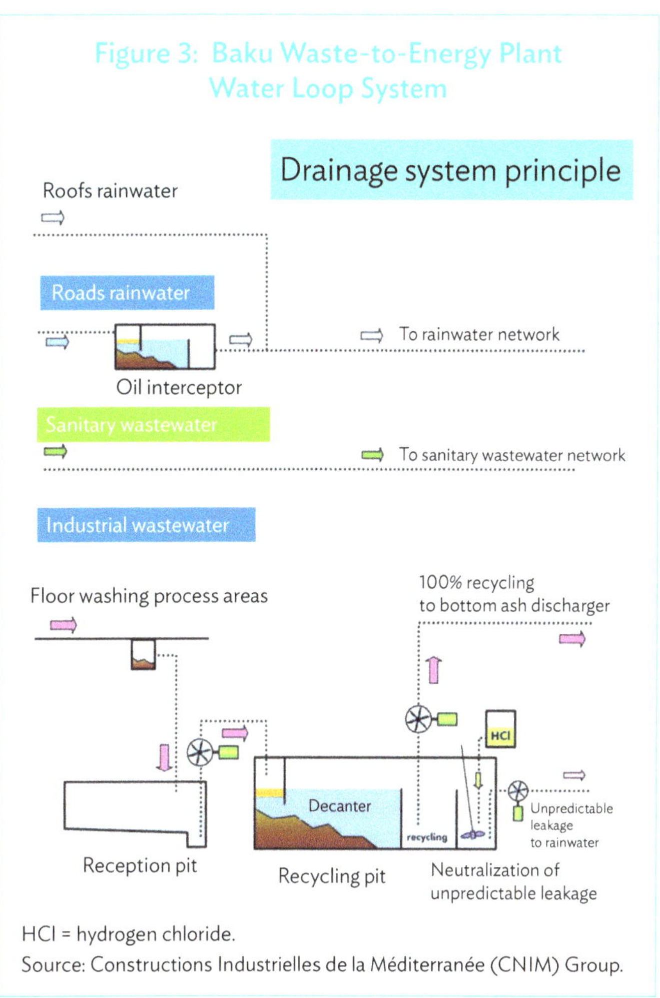

Figure 3: Baku Waste-to-Energy Plant Water Loop System

HCl = hydrogen chloride.
Source: Constructions Industrielles de la Méditerranée (CNIM) Group.

BUSINESS MODEL

Waste treatment and disposal in Baku are managed by state-owned company Tamiz Shahar JSC, under the auspices of the Ministry of Economy and Industry. The company is responsible for construction, commissioning, and operation of landfill disposal, treatment, and recovery facilities in Greater Baku Area, including the Baku WtE Plant.

This public company recovers the investment through the following revenue streams: electricity sales, waste treatment services, and subsidies from the government to offset low collection and treatment tariffs.

FINANCING STRUCTURE

The Government of Azerbaijan represented by the Ministry of Economy and the Islamic Development Bank financed the construction of the Baku WtE Plant. The ministry initiated the project but Tamiz Shahar took over the ownership of the plant in 2008. Tamiz Shahar has the sole authority on solid waste disposal and utilization in Baku area.

RESULTS

The Baku WtE Plant has been an exemplary model of effective solid waste management in the region considering the complex solid waste management of the city. The plant has been operational since its commissioning date and was able to meet the expected outcomes of the project. Table 2 shows the performance indicators of the project from 2013–2019.

Table 2: Performance Indicators of Baku Waste-to-Energy Project

Production Year	Waste Received (Tonnes)	Waste Incinerated (%)	Energy Produced (MWh)	Scrap Metal Recovered (Tonnes)
2013	369,141	99	134,080	3,430
2014	437,761	100	173,742	2,441
2015	509,370	100	181,850	3,840
2016	462,209	100	174,490	6,768
2017	463,627	100	170,330	3,317
2018	501,306	100	136,036	6,201
2019	512,492	100	164,396	5,441

MWh = megawatt-hour.
Source: Constructions Industrielles de la Méditerranée (CNIM) Group.

In 2018, the CNIM Azerbaijan Baku WtE Plant has successfully passed a supervisory audit, confirming the compliance of its Health Safety and Environmental Management System with requirements of the ISO 14001:2015 and OHSAS 18001:2007 international standards.

In parallel, Tamiz Shahar has also improved material recycling from waste with the construction of Balakhani sorting plant. This material recovery facility has an annual capacity of 200,000 tons and is constructed and operated to develop household waste segregation and recycling business in the country. As a result of sorting, paper, glass, plastic, nonferrous metal, iron, and other recyclable materials are segregated; total volume of waste is reduced; and background for establishment of recycling industry in the country is created. Additionally, hazardous waste such as batteries, accumulators, and electronic waste are separated from general waste and are sent to proper places.

LESSONS

Based on the analysis prepared for National Strategy, the solid waste composition of the power plant consists of 55% organic wastes, 28% dry recyclables, and 17% other wastes. Just like in other cities, the main issue is the lack of waste segregation scheme at source. Baku garbage has high proportion of food wastes resulting to a high moisture content, especially during summer seasons, when vegetables and fruits are widely available and consumed in large quantities. The plant has assumed a calorific value 6,000 kJ/kg –9,000 kJ/kg for burning of wastes. However, based on actual condition, heating value was only 4,500 kJ/kg –6,000 kJ/kg, hence affecting the plant's electricity production.

Despite the unfavorable composition of the municipal wastes and high moisture content, the plant's environmental performance strictly complies with European Union directive on industrial emissions and incineration of waste, and the laws pertaining to the environmental protection. Atmospheric emissions are far below the set limits owing to proper flue gas treatment technology and its continuous emissions monitoring systems. The European Commission mentions these processes as BAT. European standards are also considered as the most advanced regulations in the world for this WtE activity, which has to fulfill the most stringent emissions limits compared to any other industrial sectors.

The climate change impact is another crucial environmental point, which has been improved by replacing landfilling disposal by this WtE treatment. Municipal waste landfills have significant impact on global warming as it produces high quantity of the powerful greenhouse gas (GHG), methane. The project is reducing GHG emissions by avoiding landfill methane emissions that otherwise would be released by the landfill to the atmosphere. It also will reduce CO_2 emissions emitted by the grid due to the displacement of fossil fuel on the grid.

THE DEVELOPER

Founded in 1856, CNIM is a French equipment manufacturer and industrial contractor operating worldwide. The group provides products and services to major public and private sector organizations especially the environment, energy, defense, and technology sectors.

CNIM specializes in waste treatment and WtE solutions. It provides services to local authorities, public service contractors, and waste treatment operators. It designs, builds, and operates turnkey plants for the treatment of household wastes and nonhazardous commercial and industrial wastes.

KEYWORDS

Landfill, waste-to-energy, Baku waste-to-energy project, boiler, steam generator, flue gas, municipal solid wastes

FURTHER READING

Constructions Industrielles de La Méditerranée (CNIM). 2009. *CNIM Group and the Azerbaijani State Launch the Construction of a Waste-to-Energy Plant in Baku, First Contract of CNIM Group in this Country.* https://cnim.com/en/media/cnim-group-and-azerbaijani-state-launch-construction-waste-energy-plant-baku-first-contract.

Waste Management World. 2011. *Waste-to-Energy Plans Move Forward in Azerbaijan.* https://waste-management-world.com/a/waste-to-energy-plans-move-forward-in-azerbaijan.

Clean Development Mechanism (CDM), UNFCCC. 2012. *Baku Waste-to-Energy Project PDD Version 4.* Bonn: United Nations Framework Convention on Climate Change. https://cdm.unfccc.int/Projects/DB/RINA1349852899.64/view.

US Energy Information Administration. n.d. *Energy Explained.* https://www.eia.gov/energyexplained/?page=biomass_waste_to_energy.

Best Available Techniques (BAT) Reference Document for Waste Incineration. https://ec.europa.eu/jrc/en/publication/eur-scientific-and-technical-research-reports/best-available-techniques-bat-reference-document-waste-incineration-industrial-emissions.

1.2 Pilot Project Waste to Energy with Bio-Drying

CONTEXT

Indonesia is one of the largest generators of MSW in the Asia and Pacific region. With waste management infrastructure in its infancy, pollution of atmosphere, soils, and waters is severe.

With a population of 250 million people, about 185,000 tons of waste is produced daily or an equivalent of 67 million tons per year (2017). The amount of waste grows annually at the rate of 2% to 3%. Seventy percent of this waste goes to 200 final disposal sites, of which less than 20 sites are sanitary landfills.

The capital city of Jakarta alone generates approximately 9,300 tons of MSW per day, but only two-thirds (approximately 6,200 tons) are collected and landfilled. The energy lost in the landfilled waste would be sufficient to provide electricity to 570,000 middle-class households.

The development of cement industry is one of the keys to economic and social development. It provides important base materials for construction of housing, transport,

PROJECT SUMMARY

PROJECT NAME:
Pilot Project Waste to Energy with Bio-Drying

CAPITAL COST:
$300,000

DEVELOPER:
Indocement

PROJECT HOST:
Indocement

GEOGRAPHICAL LOCATION:
Citeureup, West Java, Indonesia

TYPE OF ENERGY PROJECT:
Municipal Solid Waste for Combustion

PROJECT COMPLETION YEAR:
2012

Indocement Citeureup Plant. The Citeureup plant located in southwest of Jakarta, West Java showcased the use of bio-drying to convert wet municipal solid waste organics into fuel with a heat equal to wood (photo by Indocement)

communication, power, and water infrastructure, among others. However, cement production is highly energy-intensive. The production of 1 ton of Portland cement consumes about 1,700 megajoules (MJ) of energy. Most of the required energy is provided by burning coal, contributing to global warming.

In the past decade, Indocement and its parent group Heidelberg Cement are targeting to replace coal with alternative fuels including refuse-derived fuel (RDF). Heidelberg Cement has many plants throughout the world that highly utilize alternative fuels.

SOLUTION

In 2014, PT Indocement Tunggal Prakarsa Tbk started an Alternative Fuel (AF) Pilot Project in its Citeureup plant located in southwest of Jakarta, West Java (Figure 5). The pilot project aims to find the best technical solution to reduce the moisture content of fresh MSW to serve as a suitable coal replacement for the cement plant's kiln operation.

Unlike in Europe where RDF materials and organics are separated at source, wastes in Indonesia are not properly segregated. To just recover RDF materials while dumping all the rest in the open does not reduce the pollution of the environment. The MSW organic fraction left in open dumps continue to release methane and carbon dioxide into the atmosphere. Heavy metal, chemical, and disease-contaminated leachate would still pollute soils, fields, and groundwater. To address these issues, PT Indocement selected a technology that not only provides alternative fuels, but improves public health and environmental protection as well.

The bio-drying process combines recovery of RDF from fresh MSW and the provision of public sanitation by stopping all waste-related emissions. In contrast to typical RDF recovery projects, bio-drying turns all combustible materials, as well as the MSW organic fraction, into fuel. It recovers materials for recycling and can bring the volume that needs to go to landfill to zero. The heat for

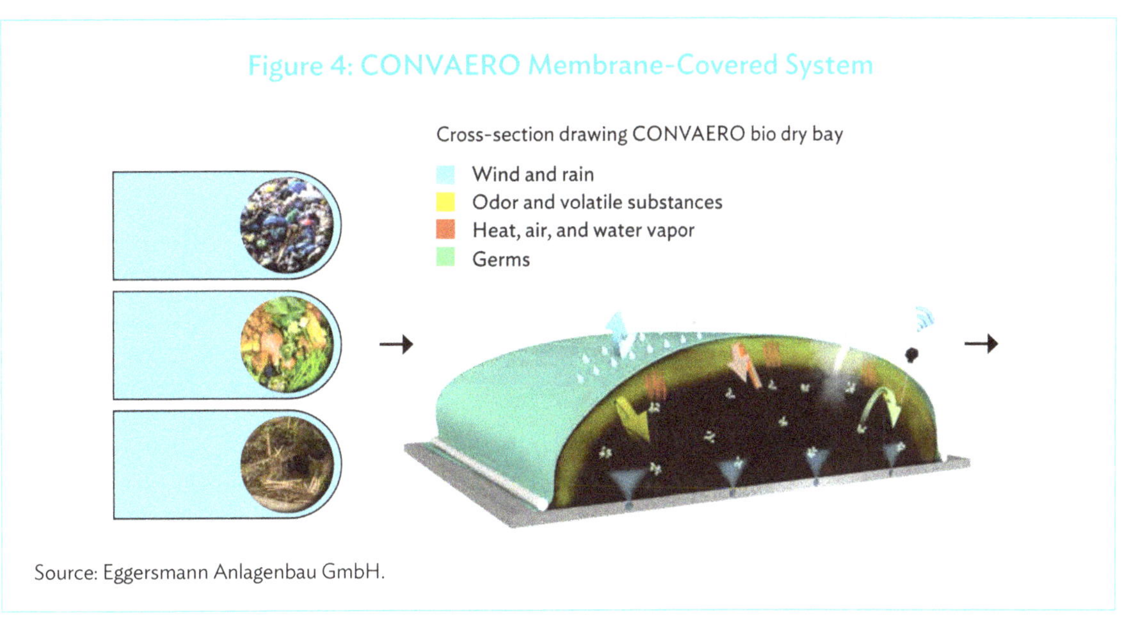

Source: Eggersmann Anlagenbau GmbH.

drying is generated not by fuel, but by heat of the organic material contained in the waste. Hence, the objective of the mechanical process is to provide optimum conditions for the bacteria to digest organics and evaporate moisture, or leachate. Figure 6 shows the cross section drawing of CONVAERO system for bio-drying.

MSW leachate is heavily contaminated with harmful bacteria, toxic chemicals, and heavy metals, and it is nearly impossible to reduce contamination to the legally acceptable discharge level using traditional wastewater treatment system. Therefore, evaporating the moisture (leachate) is a perfect solution. Contaminants that remain in the fuel are destroyed in the combustion process. The flue gas-filtering and ash-handling system captures the residue of this process for safe final disposal.

In bio-drying, the waste is homogenized by shredding. All plastic bags, boxes, bottles, and containers are opened to release their organic content. The material is then put on windrows and force aerated with fans from below the ground forcing oxygen into the material to sustain aerobic bacteria. Their metabolic activity slowly heats up the entire material up to 70°C over 21 days, killing most biological pathogens. The semipermeable cover allows moisture to evaporate into the atmosphere, but blocks rainwater from infiltrating into the material.

TECHNOLOGY

The MSW of most Asian countries consists of 50%–70% fresh organic materials. It is full of active bacteria that metabolize organics to energy, water, and CO_2-inhaling oxygen called aerobic bacteria.

However, if waste is stacked, large parts of the heap become anaerobic as no oxygen can enter in between the materials. Aerobic bacteria would die and anaerobic bacteria that do not require oxygen to live degrade the materials, thereby releasing methane, which is a GHG, 21 times more harmful than CO_2.

CONVAERO Bio-Dry System. This is a membrane covered system for composting and biological drying of waste (photo by Indocement)

Bio-drying actively pumps air into the material to supply aerobic bacteria with oxygen. The temperature of the bacteria heats up the entire heap up to 70°C. The high temperature evaporates water and kills germs harmful to humans. After 14–21 days retention time, 60%–70% of the original mass is lost. Moisture drops from 60%–70% to 25%–35%.

The pilot project was largely manually operated to test the efficiency of the drying system. After receiving and weighing the waste, it was stacked and covered for subsequent aeration. After two to three turns, the dry material was then transported, shredded, and fed into the calciner of the cement plant. Figure 7 shows the CONVAERO bio-dry system.

The results of trial tests revealed that 95% of the waste was either evaporated or turned into fuel. Only a small portion of leachate and hazardous or inert materials need final disposal.

Figure 5: Complete Process

Source: Indocement.

BUSINESS MODEL

The overall objective of the project is to substitute coal by waste as fuel. The owner of the pilot project and facilities is Indocement. High moisture content dramatically reduces the heating value of MSW as fuel. The pilot project aimed to verify whether bio-drying is a viable way to reduce this moisture content. Once successful, Indocement could then introduce the technology and concept to local regulators and interested parties for large-scale project implementation.

The pilot project ran from October 2014 to May 2017. During this period, various batches of local waste were processed over a 21-day period. Results from the pilot plant will be used for conceptualizing future large-scale projects. Figure 8 illustrates the complete process from delivery of MSW to burning in calciner.

mm = millimeter, MSW = municipal solid waste, RDF = refuse-derived fuel.
Source: Indocement.

The project was successful in testing at smaller scale with lesser cost, that can be replicated in an industrial scale. The total investment of $300,000 was financed solely by Indocement. The cost included engineering, civil works, and equipment such as blowers, membrane covers, and electrical controls for two bays that could hold 100 tons of fresh MSW each. Alternative fuel is widely used in the cement industry worldwide. However, fuel made from wet Indonesia MSW by bio-drying can be cheaper than the equivalent energy from coal but also depends on the waste tipping fee paid.

RESULTS

As shown in Figure 9, the pilot project proved that bio-drying can

(i)   reduce the moisture content of Indonesian MSW from 60% to 20% within a period of approximately 21 days,

(ii) increase the very low heating value of the fresh MSW to a heating value of wood as replacement for coal,

(iii) help reduce the carbon footprint of cement production by substituting part of the coal burned with bio-dried waste as fuel,

(iv) stop or avoid fresh MSW-related emissions such as the contaminated leachate from waste and GHGs such as methane, and

(v)   provide public sanitation by destroying harmful chemical compounds and disease vectors burning them in the cement kiln.

LESSONS

Microbe activity plays a key role in the function of the mechanical–biological treatment system, so all conditions have to be optimized for growth and full function.

Moisture content of the waste changes with the seasons and also festivities and holidays. As a consequence, times needed for drying vary. This needs to be taken into account when planning the fuel composition in cement production throughout the year.

Opening closed plastic bags by shredding is essential to release all contained organics. Hazardous and inert materials need to be minimized, because they can delay the biological process. Biotoxic chemicals can even stop the process.

Mixing the material by wheel loader has proven ineffective and costly especially in larger-scale operations due to lack of efficiency. In the pilot phase, turning needed 5 to 8 hours with extra space for maneuvering. In larger facilities, turning machines that are used for compost might have better potential and should be studied carefully.

The mechanical–biological treatment of MSW on industrial scale as targeted by Indocement offers good quality, and long-term employment opportunity for local community.

The biological process and handling of fresh waste can release odors. Location should be considered and close collaboration with local community is necessary. Bio-drying facilities should be placed in noncritical areas, e.g., landfill or industrial zones should be far from settlements.

Typical RDF recovery systems only target high-heating value materials such as plastics; rubber; and paper, cardboard, or wood.

All other materials remain unused including the large "organic" fraction. The term organic does not mean this material is harmless or food grade. In reality it is highly contaminated with chemicals and heavy metals, and carries diseases. Its applicability as compost or fertilizer depends on the level of contamination.

Bio-drying converts wet MSW organics into fuel with a heat value equal to wood. Burning it in cement kilns then destroys disease carriers and harmful chemicals.

THE DEVELOPER

Indocement is one of the leaders within the Indonesian cement, aggregate, and concrete industries. The company is part of the international Heidelberg Cement Group, the second-largest cement producer in the world. All of its worldwide cement production plants aim to reduce the consumption of primary energy by the use of alternative fuels prepared from local waste materials. The specific challenge in the Asia and Pacific region is the very high moisture content of its MSW. Therefor a drying system was needed. Bio-drying was selected because the drying heat does not come from fuel burned, but from the body temperature of the bacteria decomposing organic waste materials.

KEYWORDS

MSW, municipal solid waste, RDF, refuse-derived fuel, alternative fuel, cement plant, HeidelbergCement, Indocement, MBT, moisture, mechanical–biological treatment, aerobic bacteria

FURTHER READING

Tom, A.P., R. Pawels, and A. Haridas. 2016. *Biodrying Process: A Sustainable Technology for Treatment of Municipal Solid Waste with High Moisture Content.* https://www.ncbi.nlm.nih.gov/pubmed/26774396.

Indocement. 2020. *Indocement: The Indonesian Project Developer.* [In Bahasa] http://www.indocement.co.id/v5/id/.

HeidelberCement Group. n.d. *Indocement's The Global Parent Company.* https://www.heidelbergcement.com/en.

CONVAERO. n. d. *The Products of CONVAERO–Drying is Key.* https://wasteconcepts.cleaner-production.de/images/cro/11-CONVAERO_Sales_Services_GmbH.pdf.

1.3 Decentralized Plastic Pyrolysis

CONTEXT

Virudhunagar is an agricultural center in southeastern Tamil Nadu. Waste management has been a challenge for the municipality administration, particularly from its vegetable market.

In Virudhunagar, plastic was dumped on the streets with a limited amount being collected and sent to landfills. This lack of sanitation created numerous problems including:

(i)   blockage of the drainage system,

(ii) stoppage of rainwater/water source recharge, and

(iii) accumulation of water in ponds allowing dengue mosquito to breed.

The unhygienic situation continues to be a problem for the people of Virudhunagar. The waste was difficult to manage for several reasons.

<table>
<tr><td colspan="2">PROJECT SUMMARY</td></tr>
<tr><td>PROJECT NAME:</td><td>Decentralized Plastic Pyrolysis</td></tr>
<tr><td>CAPITAL COST:</td><td>$4,300 (₹300,000)[3]</td></tr>
<tr><td>DEVELOPER:</td><td>Caring Nature</td></tr>
<tr><td>PROJECT HOST:</td><td>Jeypee Farm, Panai Nagar</td></tr>
<tr><td>GEOGRAPHICAL LOCATION:</td><td>Virudhunagar, Tamil Nadu, India</td></tr>
<tr><td>TYPE OF ENERGY PROJECT:</td><td>Waste to Energy Plastic Waste to Fuel Oil</td></tr>
<tr><td>PROJECT COMPLETION YEAR:</td><td>2018</td></tr>
</table>

It was contaminated and pretreatment was required for recycling items, especially plastics.

There was no market price for plastics and there were reprocessing issues due to the variety of plastics that are mixed together. There was insufficient space near the market.

Figure 10 shows the various processes in managing the waste from collection to vermi-composting of market wastes and pyrolysis of plastics.

Caring Nature, a local environmental nongovernment organization, took the initiative to develop a WtE pilot plant for vegetable market waste. This involved composting the homogeneous organic market waste and converting plastics to fuel oil through pyrolysis. Caring Nature provided a decentralized plastic pyrolysis system for handling segregated plastic waste. Jeypee Farms provided the vermi-composting materials and the project demonstrated that a new circular economy in Virudhunagar was possible.

---

[3]   1$:69.76 Indian rupees as of December 2018 (Source: https://forex.adb.org/fx_rate/getRates).

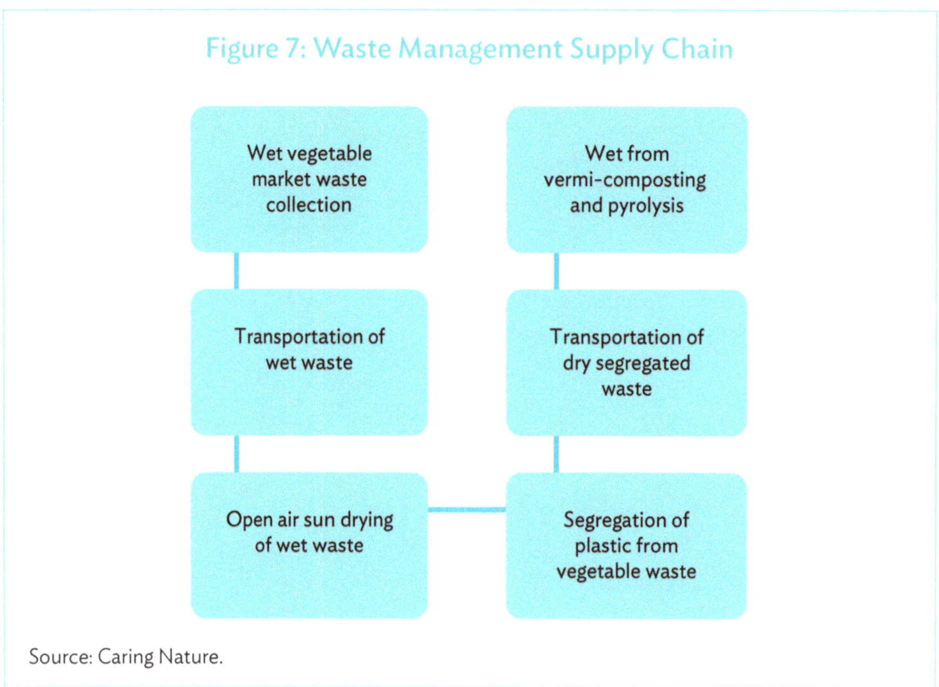

Source: Caring Nature.

SOLUTION

Vegetable market vendors were consulted through their trade association and citizens' forum. They were encouraged to segregate the vegetable waste and hand them over to municipal authority workers. Waste collection bags were provided to all vegetable market traders for easy and efficient collection. An awareness drive was made to reach out to individual waste generator and they are tracked using a database.

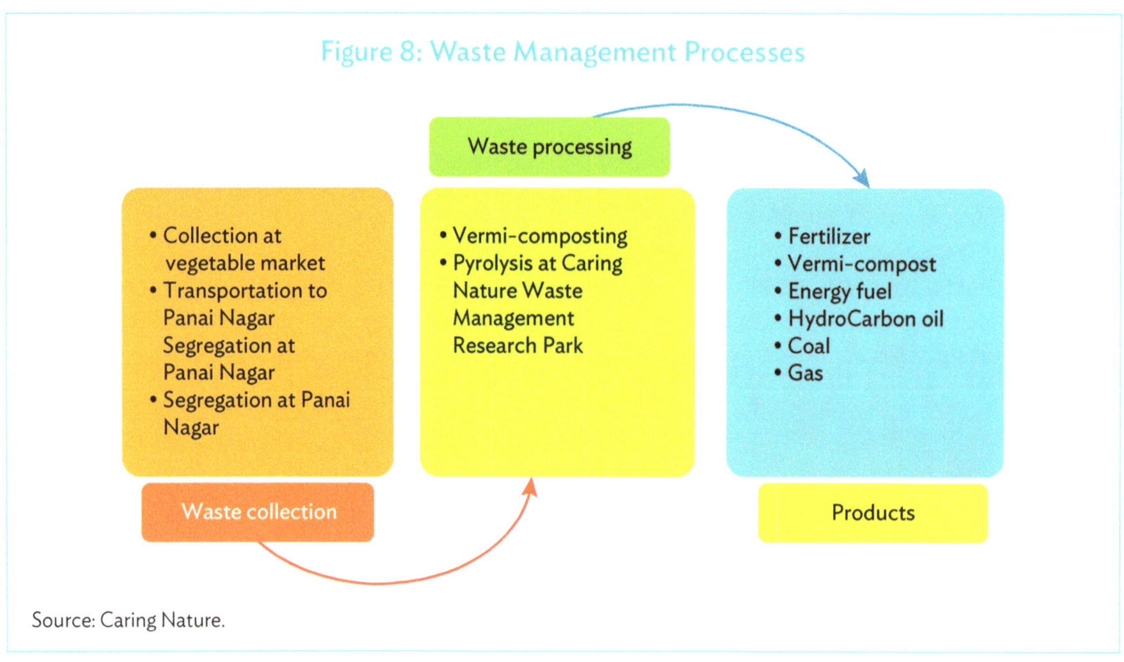

Source: Caring Nature.

Collection of vegetable wastes from the market was the responsibility of the municipality. Depending on the quantity of wastes generated, two to four municipal workers spend 1 to 3 hours daily. They use a tricycle to do primary segregation and transfer the waste to a collection vehicle.

A Caring Nature vehicle carried all the wastes collected from vegetable market to its own resource recovery center at Panai Nagar Resource Recovery Park, approximately 2 kilometers from the vegetable market. The vegetable market wastes are usually wet with high moisture content (>60%), which is reduced through open-air sun drying. Figure 11 shows the waste management processes while Figure 12 illustrates waste management practices of Caring Nature.

Waste Management Practices. Caring Nature collected the wastes from vegetable markets to its own resource recovery center at Panai Nagar Resource Recovery Park (photo by Caring Nature).

TECHNOLOGY

Sun-dried plastic waste and other non-compostable materials were separated manually using simple forked hand tools. Jeypee Biotech took the segregated compostable materials and the non-compostable plastic wastes were turned over to Caring Nature. The technologies used were

    (i)   vermi-composting in tanks using Jeypee Eisenia foetida earth worm for vegetable waste, and

    (ii)   zero-electricity, batch type decentralized plastic pyrolysis using woods from village for non-compostable materials.

The mixed vegetable market waste contained plastics of different types. Plastics have high-energy compounds and energy in the plastics can be recovered through pyrolysis. This technology converts mixed waste plastics into fuel oil, which can be used in furnaces.

The technology is designed and made in India. It is intended for use by local villagers using local available resources. Caring Nature is currently applying for technology patent.

Batch Type Decentralized Plastic Pyrolysis. Through this pyrolysis system, the energy gained was 173,791 kilocalories (kCal) with the efficiency of 47.2% (photo by Caring Nature).

Energy Balance

Pyrolysis is a process of indirect heating of the substance in the absence of oxygen in a controlled manner. The process requires energy to produce the energy resources including fuel oil, carbon residue, and flammable gas. Firewood is used for initial ignition. Figure 13 shows the vessel for pyrolysis. The energy balance of the system and its efficiency are shown in Table 3 below:

Table 3: Energy Balance

Input Energy	Output Energy
Firewood 100 kgs (for processing 98 kgs of plastic waste) 100 kgs *2000 kcal/kg = 200,000 kCal	Hydrocarbon oil 49 kgs 49 kgs*7041 kcal/kg = 345,009 kcal Carbon residue 11.7 kgs 11.7 kgs*2460 kcal/kg = 28,782 kcal
	Total energy generated = 373,791 kcal

kCal = kilocalorie, kg = kilogram.
Source: Caring Nature.

Through this pyrolysis system, the energy gained was 373,791 kilocalories (kCal) with the efficiency of 47.2%. The firewood that is used for initial ignition can be replaced with hydrocarbon gas (equivalent to liquefied petroleum gas [LPG]), which is produced by the system resulting to an increase in the efficiency level of 60% (Table 4).

Table 4: Mass Balance

Reactant (kgs)	Products	Percentage	Application
Plastic waste – 98 kgs.	Hydrocarbon oil (64 liters) Carbon residue (11.7 kgs) Hydrocarbon gas	50% 12% 38%	Furnace oil, solvent applications Heating applications Used for plastic to oil process

kgs = kilograms.
Source: Caring Nature.

The 38% uncondensed hydrocarbon gas produced is used for achieving temperature of 350°C–500°C in the 250-liter capacity pyrolyzer (Table 5).. This flammable hydrocarbon gas resource substitutes around 60% of energy consumption for running the pyrolysis process successfully.

Table 5: Result Specification

No	Description	Value
1.	Fuel Oil Characters: Density Viscosity Calorific value Moisture content Carbon: Hydrogen (%)	0.9051 g/cc 95 cSt 7,041 kCal/kg 1.3% 89 : 11
2.	Carbon residue powder Calorific value	2,460 kCal/kg

cSt = centistokes, cc= cubic centimeter, g = gram, kCal = kilocalorie, kg = kilogram.
Source: Caring Nature.

BUSINESS MODEL

With the decentralized model, the cost of transport has been greatly reduced and local laborers can be hired. One trained laborer can operate the decentralized pyrolyzer. No electricity is required and initial ignition can be done with some firewood. The cost in Virudhunagar vegetable market wastes were standardized for the weight of wet wastes collected. The associated costs are presented in Table 6.

The pyrolysis oil is being sold for Rs20 ($0.292) per liter, while the compost is being sold for Rs10 ($ 0.146) per kilogram (kg). The capital cost is less than Rs400,000 ($5,8743). Payback period is estimated at 2.5 years. It is feasible to earn around Rs300 ($5) per day, which is sufficient for the livelihood of an adult in rural India.

Table 6: Associated Costs in Processing Vegetable Market
Waste in Virudhunagar

Process	Cost Per Kg (Rs)	Cost Per Kg ($)
Collection	0.63	0.009
Open yard drying and segregation	0.82	0.012
Transport	0.74	0.011
Vermi-composting	0.40	0.005
Pyrolysis	0.31	0.004
Total	2.84	0.041

kg = kilogram, Rs = Indian rupees.
Source: Caring Nature.

FINANCING STRUCTURE

Due to low capital cost of this solution, complex financial structures are not necessary. Support for villagers, through government and large corporations' equipment leasing, would be the fastest way to roll out the technology.

RESULTS

The project has invigorated the local community. Seeing a locally made solution gave a positive impact on the thinking of the residents. The major impacts are presented in Figure 14.

The district collector and the District Rural Development Agency commended the pilot. The district collector recommended that the local government provide funding to nearby villages to use the same approach.

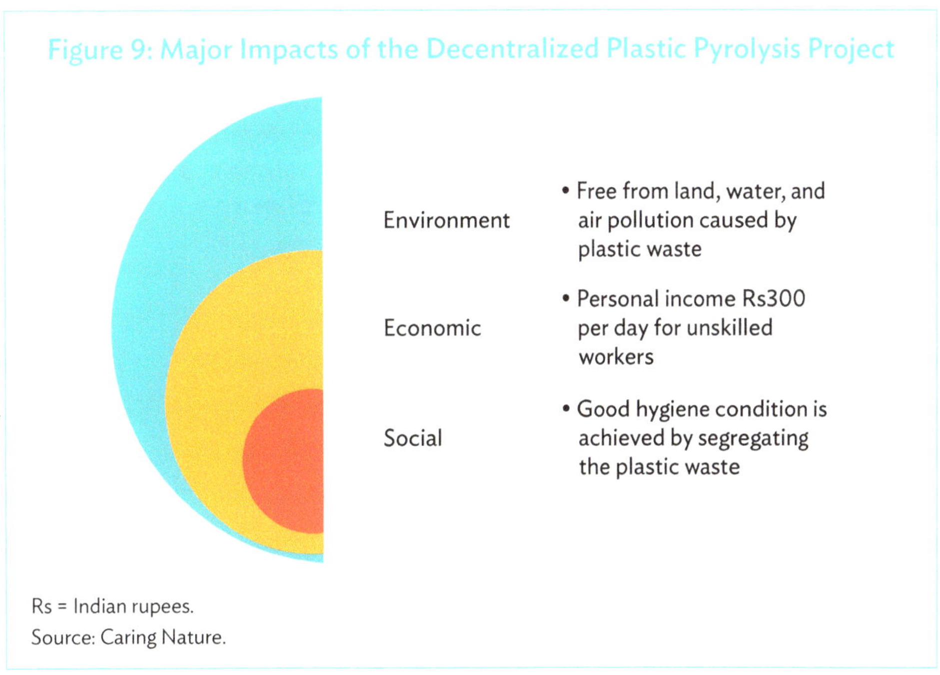

Rs = Indian rupees.
Source: Caring Nature.

The pilot demonstrated the following:

(i) Through proper waste disposal and handling techniques, resources are recovered, preventing animals to eat plastics, maintaining cleanliness of the surrounding, and minimize drainage blockage.

(ii) The prevention of open burning reduces the release of toxic dioxins, furans, and carbon monoxide which may cause respiratory ailments and affect the human immune system.

(iii) The project is economically viable and has generated employment opportunities to the local villagers.

(iv) Plastic can be removed from the environment and the system prevents the dumping of such waste in rivers and oceans.

LESSONS

Through the pilot, Caring Nature has arrived at the following estimates during project implementation:

(i) Collection – 16,195 kgs of waste collected at the rate of Rs0.54 ($0.008) per kg of wet waste

(ii) Primary transport costs – Rs0.62 ($0.01) per kg from collection point to recover site, which is around 2 kilometers

(iii) Sun drying – 1 square meter area can dry 53.72 kgs of wet waste for 27 days

(iv) Segregation – Cost is Rs0.82 ($0.012) per kg of wet waste

(v) Secondary transport – Cost is Rs0.13 ($0.002) per kg of wet waste from recovery site to composting site, which is around 8 kilometers

THE DEVELOPER

Caring Nature is an environmental nongovernment organization that aims to combat environmental hazard, improve solid waste management and climate change, and promote environmental awareness. Caring Nature's Research Wing supported the piloting of a decentralized approach toward plastic waste management led by S. Nandhagopal (Nandha). Nandha has been working in plastic pyrolysis since 2006. He designed the decentralized plastic pyrolysis plant—a novel rural and semi-urban wastes management solution.

KEYWORDS

Decentralized plastic pyrolysis, wet waste, vermi-composting, Caring Nature, hydrocarbon oil

FURTHER READING

Caring Nature. [Facebook page]. https://m.facebook.com/caringnature.org/?tsid=0.100382239372931 89&source=result.

The Hindu. 2018 Special Talent Programme. https://www.thehindu.com/todays-paper/tp-national/tp-tamilnadu/special-talent-programme/article24568188.ece.

1.4   Plastic-to-Liquid Fuel

CONTEXT

Plastics are an important material in our economy. Modern daily life is unthinkable without plastics. At the same time however, they can have serious downsides on the environment and health. The global plastic production has increased over the years due to the vast applications of plastics in many sectors. The continuous demand of plastics caused the plastic wastes accumulation in the landfill, which consumed a lot of spaces that contributed to the environmental problem. About 38 % of all plastic waste in Europe ends up in landfills, and only 26% is recycled. The remainder is utilized for energy recovery. According to the World Bank, plastic waste corresponds to 7–14 percentage weight of MSW in Asia and due to absence of waste recovery solutions, the majority of these end up in landfills.

Some alternatives have been developed to manage plastic wastes recycling and energy recovery method. However, there were some drawbacks of the recycling method as it required high labor cost for the separation process and caused water contamination that reduced the sustainability of the process. Due to these drawbacks, researchers have diverted their attention to the energy recovery method to compensate for the high-energy demand. One of the solutions is pyrolysis, or thermal decomposition (depolymerization). The technology is mature and has been applied to many different organic mixes. However, its applications have some profound limitations that need to be harnessed.

Process knowledge in combination with the right conditions is essential to make pyrolysis meaningful and profitable. Thermocatalytic tests showed that different zeolites and nickel-molybdenum catalysts was suitable in order to upgrade the quality of the decomposition product mixture. Pyrolysis with an efficient catalyst can be very efficient in converting waste plastics into pyrolysis oil, and later refined to commercial, drop-in diesel fuel.

SOLUTION

In search of available processes for production of low-carbon fuel from waste, pyrolysis of plastic was found as a viable option. Research showed that the most promising results came from batch pyrolysis units with suitable catalytic reforming of the pyrolysis oil in order to create fuel of acceptable quality. During 2016–2017, ScandGreen Energy installed and commissioned a plastic-to-liquid pyrolysis plant as a demonstration pilot. The design was batch pyrolysis reactor to verify the production process, i.e.,

PROJECT SUMMARY

PROJECT NAME:
Plastic-to-Liquid Fuel

CAPITAL COST:
$600,000

DEVELOPER:
ScandGreen Energy

PROJECT HOST:
Quantafuel MX

GEOGRAPHICAL LOCATION:
Navojoa, Sonora, Mexico

TYPE OF ENERGY PROJECT:
Waste to Energy

PROJECT COMPLETION YEAR:
2017

proof-of-concept of the waste plastic-to-diesel technology and to optimize the subprocesses and the overall plant operation.

The People's Republic of China (PRC) has developed a number of successful pyrolysis processes for scrap tires and most of the manufacturers are located in the Henan province. After visiting different suppliers in October 2015, a batch pyrolysis and distillation plant was selected. The plant capacity was at 10 tons per day (TPD) of plastic, yielding around 6 TPD of diesel and a smaller fraction of gasoline, carbon, light gases, and heavy oil.

The plant was erected and modified in Navojoa, Sonora, Mexico where the project's joint venture partner had acquired land and organized operating permits.

TECHNOLOGY

From June 2016 to April 2017, it was validated that the plastic-to-liquid process via a modified pyrolysis and distillation procedure was suitable for the production of diesel of ASTM D975 quality on a demonstration scale. The process of converting plastic to liquid fuel is shown in Figure 15.

The Navojoa plant ran 20 pyrolysis batches with different plastic types and 18 distillations. It was found that pyrolysis of high-density polyethylene (HDPE) followed by three consecutive distillations of the HDPE pyrolysis oil resulted in diesel of the best quality.

The distillation scheme was done to simulate a continuous process in a distillation tower. The diesel proved to be ASTM D975-compliant, with high cetane index (60), high flash point (55°C), good boiling curve, and low polycyclic aromatic hydrocarbons (PAHs) (3.8 %). To qualify for EN590, the level of sulfur must be reduced and the oxidation stability increased. Sulfur will be low in sorted plastic and the new generation catalyst and reactor system will ensure that the oxidation stability will be EN590-compliant.

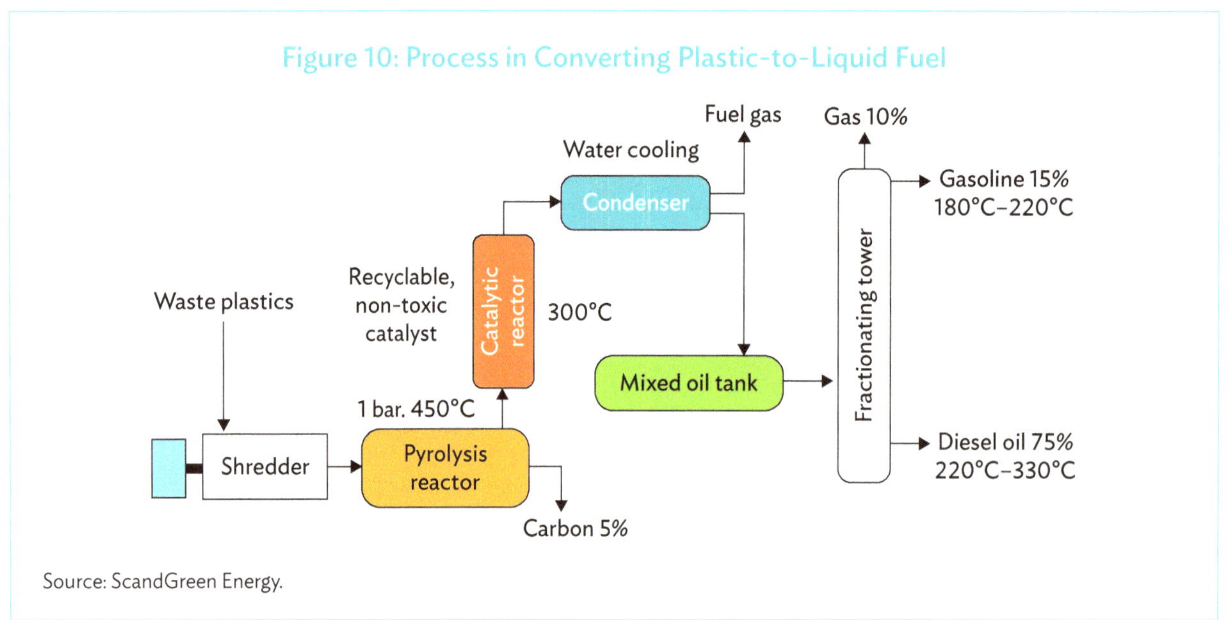

Figure 10: Process in Converting Plastic-to-Liquid Fuel

Source: ScandGreen Energy.

BUSINESS MODEL

The pilot project was developed and funded by ScanGreen Energy to test its technical and economic viability. The project was later on acquired by the host company, Quantafuel MX.

FINANCING STRUCTURE

The project capital cost amounted to $600,000 with a $60,000 yearly operation and maintenance cost. Incoming sorting was made manually by scavengers (or waste pickers) on a belt and included in the operation costs. With a 60 weight percent (wt%) converted to diesel and 90% uptime, the project gives a levelized cost of energy of $0.06 per liter of diesel produced. Depending on feedstock, the project will get some light fractions (similar to gasoline) that may be refined to benzene, toluene, or other high-end products. The heavy fraction can serve as offtake to cement industry or similar. These other products are not included in the net output since the price per unit varies depending on location. With the right off-taker, the levelized cost of energy goes down below to $0.05/liter.

RESULTS

To produce the sufficient amount of pyrolysis oil for the distillation, several pyrolysis runs had to be performed. Prior to the distillation, the mixed plastic pyrolysis oil was washed in 0.3wt% sodium hydroxide (NaOH) relative to the total oil quantity. The HDPE pyrolysis oil was washed in 1.0wt% NaOH relative to the total oil quantity.

Cetane Number and Index

The cetane number is a measure of the ignition quality of a diesel fuel. It is often mistaken as a measure of fuel quality. Cetane number is actually a measure of a fuel's ignition delay. This is the time period between the start of injection and start of combustion (ignition) of the fuel. In a particular diesel engine, higher-cetane fuels will have shorter ignition delay periods than lower-cetane fuels. A low-cetane fuel would result in difficulties starting the engine, especially cold start in winter conditions.

Besides that density, calorific value, distillation range, sulfur content, stability, and flash point are all very important. In colder weather, cloud point and low temperature filter plugging point may be critical factors. ASTM D975 determines the requirements of diesel fuel in the United States. The minimum cetane number, and also index, is set to 40, but it usually varies between 42 and 45. In a similar way, the quality of the diesel for Europe is specified by the EN 590 standard, with a minimum acceptable cetane number of 51 and a minimum cetane index of 46. Both standards specify the environmental parameters and functionality requirements. They are broadly used as reference for fuel providers in the Americas and Europe.

The flash point is an important parameter for diesel fuel as it describes the temperature when flammable light fractions are flashed off. The reason for the presence of light flammable fraction in the diesel is due to the solubility of these fractions in the diesel. It may be compared to carbon dioxide in a soda. When pressure is released (the soda is opened), gas is bubbling and released to the atmosphere. The flash point limit in ASTM D975 is 45°C, while for EN590 it is 55°C.

Analysis of Organics in Diesel

The reaction mechanism for pyrolysis of plastics shows the creation of radicals that will create aromatics and olefins in the propagation and termination steps. For choice of catalysts, it is important to focus is on the ratio between aromatics, olefins, and saturates. There are several other parameters that are important, but these components give an indication on the effect of the installed catalyst and also on the quality of plastic used.

The type of plastic has a great effect on the aromatic content. In the case of HDPE, the amount of both olefins and saturates increased and the number of aromatics decreased. This is because the aromatics are first decomposed to olefins, which are then decomposed by hydrogen to saturates.

Carbon Number Distribution

Diesel samples from distillations were analyzed by advanced petroleum technology using gas chromatography linked with a mass spectrometer (GC-MS). Initially, two analyses were done of the diesel samples.

The first identified various isomers of alkanes, cycloalkanes, and aromatics both with and without (mono-, di-, and tri-) methyl or ethyl functional groups. The second identified various PAHs with a variety of functional groups. When all PAHs that had a concentration below 100 nanogram/gram diesel were removed, a total of 40 PAHs remained, which accounted for less than 0.5wt% in both diesel samples.

To evaluate the distribution of straight-chain normal alkanes, these components were compared separately, which accounted for approximately 90% of the components identified in both diesel samples. In other words, 90wt% of the total 30wt% identified were normal alkanes with no branching or additional methyl/ethyl functional groups. The distribution of normal alkanes is shown in Figure 16, in which the concentration of the normal alkane (milligram/gram oil) is plotted against the carbon number of the normal alkane. This plot clearly shows that the majority of the normal alkanes are within C9–C21, which is consistent with the distribution normally seen in diesel fuels.

Since the first analysis by advanced petroleum technology only accounted for 30wt% of the total diesel sample, another analysis was done by quantifying the results by carbon number alone, to account for a larger fraction of the sample. This resulted in 85wt% and 92wt% being accounted for. In this case, the relative amounts of each carbon number contain all compounds with that carbon number, not just alkanes. This means that straight-chain and branched alkanes and olefins, as well as cycloalkanes and aromatics with the same carbon number, are included. The results of this analysis are shown in Figure 16, which results in a very similar distribution as the one shown in Figure 17, and is still consistent with the carbon number distribution of diesel.

A test plan was formulated to optimize the diesel fuel quality produced in the batch pyrolysis plant. The goal was to focus on improving the cetane index and flash point temperature. It was also important to analyze the aromatics, olefins, and saturates since these components gives an indication on the catalyst activity. It was found that pyrolysis oil from HDPE, use of the catalyst, and three sequential distillations gave the best diesel quality.

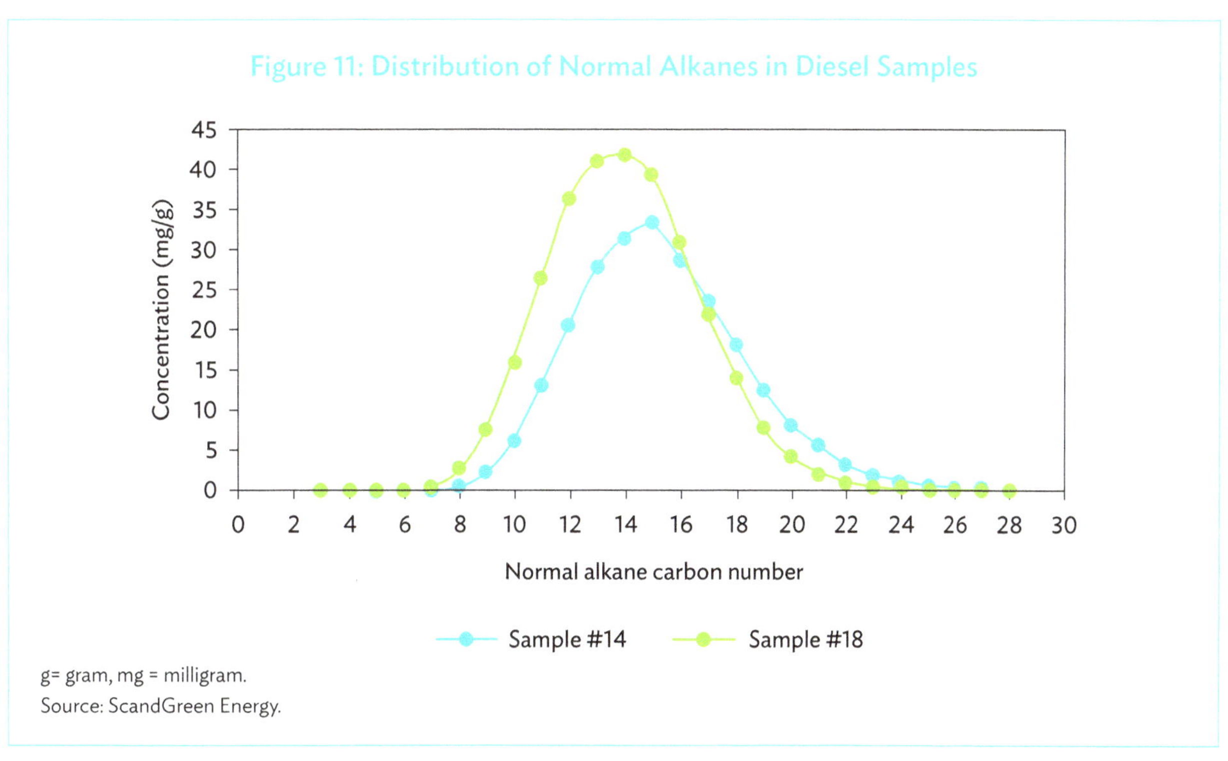

Figure 11: Distribution of Normal Alkanes in Diesel Samples

g= gram, mg = milligram.
Source: ScandGreen Energy.

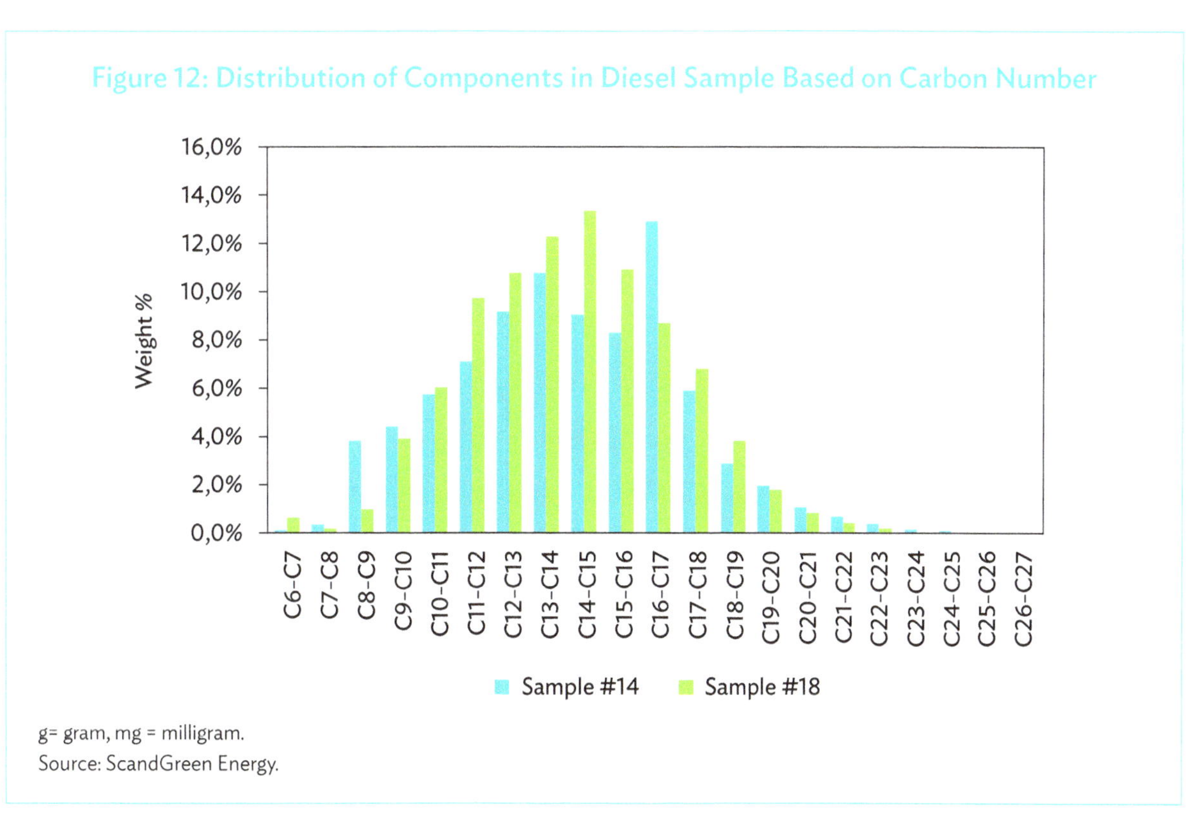

Figure 12: Distribution of Components in Diesel Sample Based on Carbon Number

g= gram, mg = milligram.
Source: ScandGreen Energy.

Monitoring shows that the diesel product becomes better for each distillation and that a diesel output complied with ASTM D975. To qualify for EN590, the sulfur content and the oxidation stability were too high. The oxidation stability is linked to both sulfur and olefins. Sulfur will only be present in small quantities using sorted plastic. The olefins present in the end product is due to the plastic being split into alkanes, olefins, carbon, and hydrogen. A catalyst that saturated olefins using available hydrogen was installed. However, the batch system is not a perfect system to install catalysts as the temperature varies over time and the catalyst is deactivated over a short period of time. This will not be the case for a continuous system.

All in all, it showed that the project was able to convert 60wt% of the waste plastic into drop-in diesel.

LESSONS

Communication is everything. The importance of communication can never be underestimated. Engineers and civil workers employed spoke four different languages and spent a lot of time and effort communicating—even assisted by professional translators. Due to cultural differences, the same level of effort was necessary to communicate with different departments including chemical engineers.

Knowledge in chemistry is fundamental. Without a solid process knowledge, the expected results could not be achieved even different equipment were installed. Constant supervision and monitoring were also necessary to get good results.

Prepare for delays and complications. Acquiring plants from the other side of the world is not something to take lightly. Close monitoring in every step on the way is critical to minimize costs and delays. Preparation and good relationship with local community are keys to this process.

Quality assurance is essential. The project was complicated and delayed by poor manufacturing standards. During the first 3 months of operation, several parts of the plant malfunctioned and had to be replaced. The burners were badly designed; notwithstanding the temperature they were exposed to. The generators were malfunctioning, the plastic shredder had too low capacity, and the exhaust gas cleaning system did not work as specified. Pumps were too small to manage the pressure drop over the installed filter, the filters were blocked after only a few minutes of operation, and the heating system was also badly designed. The overall performance like feed capacity or heating time was not according to specification and had to be tested once the plant was ready for commissioning. A performance bond based on this final stage is necessary.

The overall quality of the purchased plant was not up to standards and needed several modifications by the local crew in Navojoa. However, after the upgrade, there is a need for the plant to become operational to produce high-quality diesel fuel. Process knowledge proved to be essential in this process. The plant was ready for start-up in June 2016.

To secure the feedstock preparation, a local religious organization was engaged and waste pickers from a nearby landfill were recruited. The waste pickers were educated in waste sorting and equipped with protective clothing and put to work in very short time. This proved to be a very successful part of corporate social responsibility program providing support with a steady income for the less fortunate. In the first trials, mixed plastic was used as the raw material, but it was found that HDPE gave the optimum diesel quality.

THE DEVELOPER

ScandGreen Energy offers innovative, financially viable, and efficient solutions to reduce pollution generated by municipal solid waste, as well as agricultural residues, forestall, or stock breeding activities. ScandGreen Energy solutions include power production, thermal energy, synthetic fuels, fertilizers, and other products.

KEYWORDS

Pyrolysis, plastic-to-liquid, cetane index, ScandGreen Energy, Quantafuel MX, HDPE, pyrolysis reactor

FURTHER READING

Scandgreen Energy. *Clean and Green Energy from Organic Waste.* http://www.scandgreen.se/.

1.5   Ankur Waste-to-Energy Project

CONTEXT

MSW generation is an issue of major concern. The amount of waste being generated is proportional to the number of people. There is no real solution to this problem, particularly for small towns and cities. As human beings "develop," they produce more and more wastes. Currently, urban India's average waste generation per capita is 400 grams per day. For some of the developed nations, it is at a staggering 2,500 grams per capita per day. Figure 18 shows a typical dumping site in India.

India today collects close to 100,000 TPD of waste and this will dramatically increase with the rapid urbanization. Increasing urbanization, coupled with economic development and modern lifestyles, have created this monumental problem in the form of solid waste in urban India.

MSW collection and management has thus become one of the most difficult and expensive tasks for most municipalities and municipal corporations across the world including India. Most municipal bodies spend a substantial part of their budget on municipal waste; otherwise, it will remain a problem with no definite solution. Even when the waste is collected, limited technical solutions are available to handle the waste more effectively.

Current options include landscaping, composting, biogasification, incineration or combustion—at a larger scale. Larger cities use mostly WtE plants with focus on composting. However, composting or biogas technology are appropriate for wet feedstock. There are also some issues associated with composting as a large portion of wastes are nonbiodegradable and therefore go directly to landfill. Composting is inefficient and an expensive process is necessary to handle large quantity of nondegradable materials. Only waste with less than 4 millimeter (mm) in size is currently accepted as part of the compost, and waste larger than that must go back to landfill.

Eliminating landfills, particularly in towns and small to medium cities (population of few tens of thousands to a few hundred thousands), would require a technology to safely convert this nondegradable waste (including +4 mm size) to energy and some useful products ideally on a daily basis. In addition, composting could be more effective and less costly if waste is made of purely compostable materials.

Typical Dumping Site. India today collects close to 100,000 tonnes per day of waste and this will dramatically increase with the rapid urbanization (photo by Ankur Scientific Energy Technologies).

SOLUTION

Thus, the ideal solution is a WtE technology that will substantially reduce the volume of waste. The technology can process all types of waste and nothing will be sent to a landfill. The process should generate useful end products such as fertilizer, gas, etc., without any auxiliary fuel firing. The solution is applicable to small towns and even larger cities. For larger cities, the solution should allow decentralized processing to minimize transportation and related costs. The technology should meet the international emissions standards and should be financially viable.

TECHNOLOGY

Various technical options for safe processing and conversion of mixed feeds (paper, plastics, textiles, leather, garden waste, wastes of +4 mm size from compost, small qualities of biodegradable waste, inerts below 200 mm, etc.) were analyzed by Ankur Scientific. The choice of down draft gasification with high temperature processing to eliminate environmental issues was seen as an ideal option. However, downdraft gasifier is very feed-specific as to the type of feed, size, moisture, ash content, ash fusion, bulk density, energy density, etc. MSW feed characteristics were exactly the opposite.

A gasifier with innovative design and features was developed by Ankur Scientific to suit MSW feed, which is generally not uniform in characteristics and has many issues. Ankur MSW Gasifier is an in-house technology specially developed, for mixed MSW in India. The technology is proven through extensive trials and pilot plant operation. High temperature gasification process allows the production of clean gas that is devoid from all environmental impurities. The produced gas is suitable for power generation through engine generators or boiler-turbine generator. Char/ash is the by-product which is approximately 4% by volume of MSW being fed in the gasifier. Char/ash can be used for road construction or for enriching soil Figure 19.

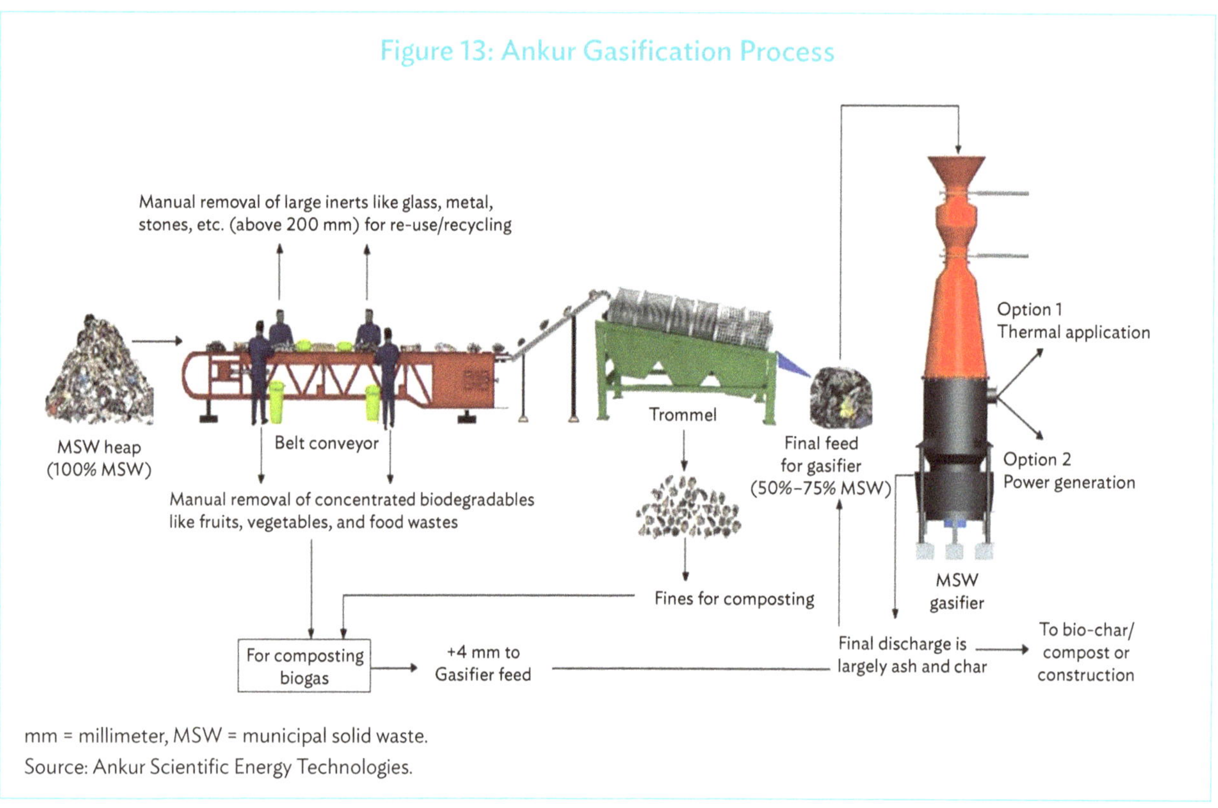

Figure 13: Ankur Gasification Process

mm = millimeter, MSW = municipal solid waste.
Source: Ankur Scientific Energy Technologies.

The types of MSW that are used in the gasifiers are garden waste, paper, cardboard, textile, plastic, leather, agri-residues, etc. The fractions of MSW that are used in the biogas plant are wet waste including food waste, fruit waste, vegetable waste, kitchen waste, concentrated food items, etc. Alternatively, it could be used in the gasifier with moisture content of less than 35%. The fractions that are not be used and required to be removed include glass, metals, building material, sand, soil, stones, etc. Figure 20 shows typical MSW.

Typical Municipal Solid Waste. Municipal solid waste collection and management becomes one of the most difficult and expensive tasks for most municipalities and municipal corporations across the world including India (photo by Ankur Scientific Energy Technologies).

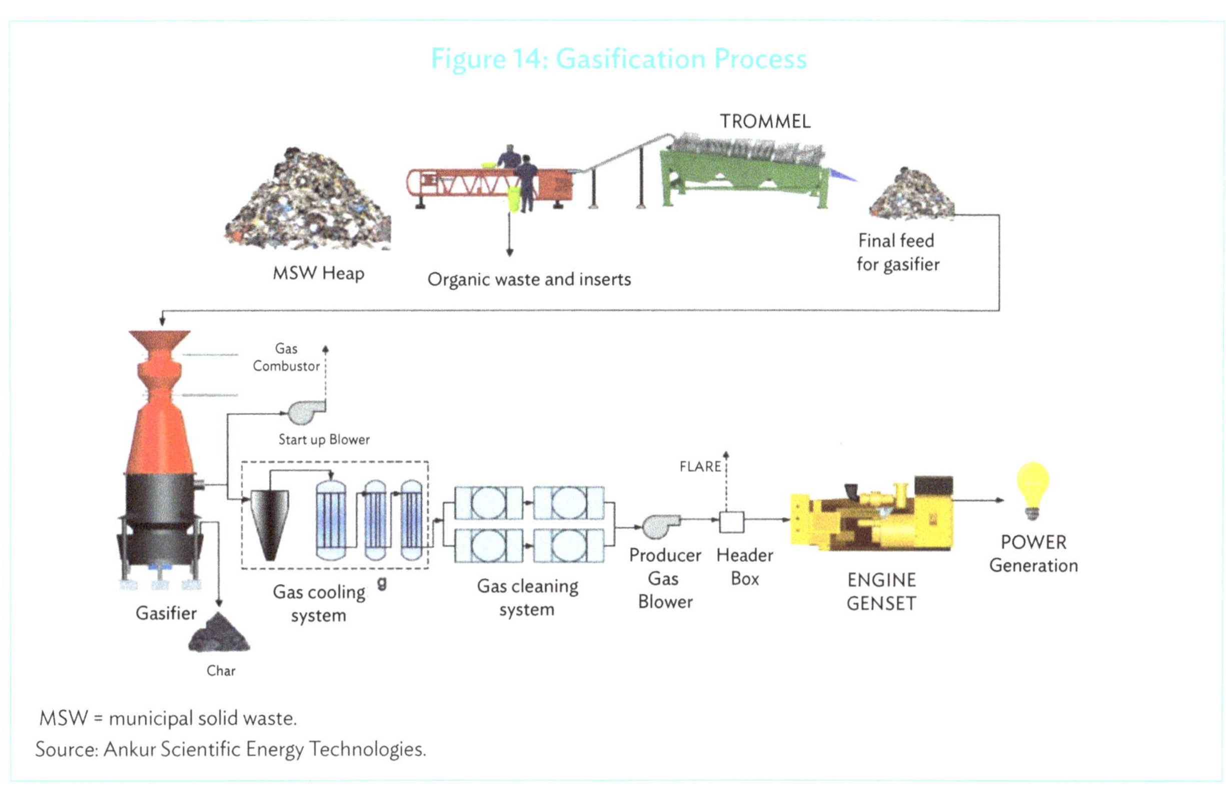

MSW = municipal solid waste.
Source: Ankur Scientific Energy Technologies.

The innovative MSW gasifier is coupled to Ankur's state-of-the-art dry gas cleaning and cooling system. The clean gas is fed to 100% producer/syngas engine as shown in Figure 21.

The pilot plant setup at Vadodara, India as shown in Figure 22 has been in operation for more than 1 year and the power generated is used by Ankur's gasifier manufacturing unit.

Pilot Plant Setup at Vadodara, India. This facility has been in operation for more than a year and the power generated is used by Ankur's gasifier manufacturing unit (photo by Ankur Scientific Energy Technologies).

Table 7 shows where Ankur's technology meets all guidelines of various state pollution control boards of India.

Table 7: Emissions of Ankur Gasification Technology

Solid Emissions	Air Emissions (at 11% O_2)* Location: Engine Exhaust		Liquid Emissions
Nontoxic ash/char generated which can be used for road building, soil enhancement, etc.	PM CO Nox + THC	< 0.2 g/kWh < 3.5 g/kWh < 4 g/kWh	System generates no liquid emissions

CO = carbon monoxide, kWh = kilowatt-hour, NOx = nitric oxide, O_2 = oxygen, PM = particular matter, THC = total hydrocarbon.
Source: Ankur Scientific Energy Technologies.

Furans and dioxin production is mainly a catalytic reaction of carbon with oxygen and chlorine in the fly ash. Dioxins and furans are strongly dependent on the type and amount of catalyst, temperature (250°C–400°C), and type and amount of carbon. Only a proper combination of all these three factors can yield dioxin and furans.

One of the advantages of gasification technology is that furans and dioxins are not formed during gasification due to the following reasons:

(i)   Lack of oxygen in reducing environment of gasifier prevents formation of free chlorine from hydrogen chloride (HCl) and limit chlorination of any precursor compounds in the gasifier.

(ii)   High temperature of gasification process effectively destroys any furan or dioxin precursor in the feed.

Construction of 50-Gigawatt Gasification Plant in Varanasi, India. This plant is the first waste-to-energy project in the city of Varanasi, India which converts 24 tonnes per day of municipal solid wastes for power generation. (photo by Ankur Scientific Energy Technologies).

Based on the success of the pilot plant, an innovative technology was commercially launched. NTPC Limited, India's largest power utility with an installed capacity of more than 50 gigawatts (GW) and expected to reach 130 GW by 2032, is setting up their first WtE project in the city of Varanasi, India. The pilot converts 24 TPD of MSW and will use Ankur's innovative MSW gasification technology. The photos during construction are shown in Figure 23.

BUSINESS MODEL

The pilot plant of Ankur Scientific was set up for demonstrating the suitability and viability of the technology for decentralized and distributed applications. Table 8 below shows the assumptions for an indicative economic analysis of a gasification technology for a small city or town generating approximately 50 TPD of dry wastes:

Table 8: Indicative Assumptions for Economic Analysis of Gasification Technology

Parameters	Approximate Amount
Total dry MSW as defined	50 tons per day
Total gross power generation	800-kWe/hour
Gross power generation @ 80% PLF	5,606,400 kWe
Internal/auxiliary power	160-kWe/hour
Net power generation	640-kWe/hour
Net power generation @ 80% PLF	4,485,120 kWe
Indicative project cost	$2.75 million
Cost of MSW	Available - free of cost
Estimated manpower cost	$107,400 year
Repairs and maintenance cost	$45,000 year
Total cost of power generation (interest not considered)	$0.034 kWe
PPA for power generation from MSW (assumed)	$0.15 kWe
Net income from sale of power	$520,368 year
Tipping fee @ $10 per ton of MSW processed (assumed)	$150,000 year
Total income from the entire plant	$670,368 year
Estimated payback period (simple payback)	~4.15 years

kWe = kilowatt electrical, PLF = plant load factor, MSW = municipal solid waste, PPA = power purchase agreement.
Source: Ankur Scientific Energy Technologies.

FINANCING STRUCTURE

For the pilot plant, the investment made by Ankur Scientific was from its internal accruals. However, to make the projects more bankable, the government has to provide incentives such as subsidies, feed-in tariffs for power sale, waste reduction and generation-based incentives, tax benefits, etc. Further, financial institutions need to provide funding and enhance affordability by offering long-term and low-interest loans.

RESULTS

The innovative and novel technology uses all fractions of MSW without extensive segregation and coupled with composting and/or biogas plants ensuring that nothing goes to landfills. Part of the in-feed is given out as totally benign ash or char that can be used for roads, buildings, etc., while the balance material is converted to gas.

The way the system is designed ensures that all emissions norms are met. The systems are designed for distributed use. Thus, the smallest system is a 25-TPD plant and the largest can handle up to 200 TPD. This means that the technology can be used in small towns as well as large cities.

LESSONS

Downdraft gasification, in general, is very feed-specific and largely depends on the characteristics and type of feed such as size, moisture, ash content, ash fusion, bulk density, energy density, etc. MSW feed characteristics were exactly opposite with issues on particle size and flow, low energy and bulk density, high moisture and ash content, and low ash fusion leading to clinkers. In addition, there is also a potential wide variation for each of these parameters. Extensive research and development with actual repeated trials helped solve these problems.

THE DEVELOPER

Ankur Scientific is a company that has been working in the field of biomass and WtE since 1986. It has been manufacturing biomass gasifiers to produce a combustible gas for thermal applications and power generation. Ankur Scientific was founded in December 1986 by Dr. B. Jain.

Ankur Scientific is seen as a world leader in this technology area and its products are marketed all over the world (it has installed systems in more than 35 countries across the globe). Ankur has designed different types of gasifier systems that can handle more than 50–60 different types of biomass, agri-residues, and wastes in some or the other forms.

After creating a niche in this segment, Ankur is now developing technologies for converting various types of wastes (e.g., empty fruit bunch, palm waste, poultry litter, waste tires, waste currency notes, fecal sludge, etc.) to energy.

KEYWORDS

Municipal solid waste, MSW, gasification, downdraft gasification, gasifier, dioxins, furans, NTPC Limited, India, Ankur Scientific, biomass, agri-residues, waste-to-energy, thermal, power, electricity, generation

FURTHER READING

Ankur. www.ankurscientific.com

1.6   HighCrest Corporation

CONTEXT

The Philippines has a massive poultry industry that is dominated by broilers and native Philippine chickens. Layer chicken farming is the third most popular poultry farming industry in the Philippines. Some of the biggest factors favoring the Filipino poultry industry are its massive population, fast-rising incomes, and a love for chicken.

As of 1 July 2017, the chicken population in the Philippines stood at 181.05 million. Despite the numerous challenges faced during the year, the chicken population grew 3.73% compared to the previous year.

Poor management of chicken manure disposal is a source of odors, water and soil contamination, and attracts flies. This has a strong impact on nearby farms in terms of livability, diseases transmission among chicken, and quality of soil and water.

Reliance from the grid for operation is a challenge for the Philippine poultry industry, in terms of access, reliability, and increasing prices.

PROJECT SUMMARY
PROJECT NAME:
HighCrest Corporation
CAPITAL COST:
$3.4 million
DEVELOPER:
IESBIOGAS srl
PROJECT HOST:
Around 1.3 million-broiler farm
GEOGRAPHICAL LOCATION:
Batangas, Philippines
TYPE OF ENERGY PROJECT:
Biogas to power
PROJECT COMPLETION YEAR:
2020

A broiler farm of 1.28 million birds (32 buildings with 40,000 birds capacity each) requires an average of 600 kilowatts (kW) of base load for its operation (mainly due to the ventilation of the buildings). Such a farm would operate on the base of at least seven growing cycles per year with a yearly manure production of approximately 7,000 metric tons.

SOLUTION

Considering the challenges of the Philippine poultry industry, the developer has designed a technical solution—a tank system biogas plant—that will substantially mitigate the social and environmental impacts of the farm allowing financial benefits to the farm owner. An existing IES biogas plant in Italy is illustrated in Figure 24.

In this prospective, a biogas plant represents the ideal solution and presents the following benefits:

(i)   Biogas can serve as baseload. It is cheaper and reliable power and can provide electricity cost savings to the farm.

(ii)   The operation of the farm after the project implementation is not negatively affected.

(iii) The biogas plant will generate solid soil conditioner and is an additional source of revenue.

(iv)   The implementation of the project will allow the disposal of the manure quickly allowing the increase in the number of cycles, i.e., up to eight cycles per year increasing the utilization of the farm.

(v)   Decreased mortality rate due to power interruptions.

(vi)   The manure will be processed right after the cleaning of the building at the end of the growing cycle: the impact of flies and odor will be minimized compared to the operations without the biogas plant.

(vii) With a proper manure management, the farmer can easily get the necessary permits and approval for the expansion of their operations.

IES Biogas Plant in Italy. One of the IES Biogas facilities installed in Italy (photo by IES Biogas).

TECHNOLOGY

In the absence of oxygen, anaerobic bacteria will degrade organic compounds. The result of this digestion process is biogas, made up mainly of methane and carbon dioxide. Figures 25 and 26 show the biogas flowchart and plant layout, respectively. Mass and energy balances are shown in Tables 9 and 10. The design key parameters are summarized in Figure 27.

Figure 15: Biogas Flowchart

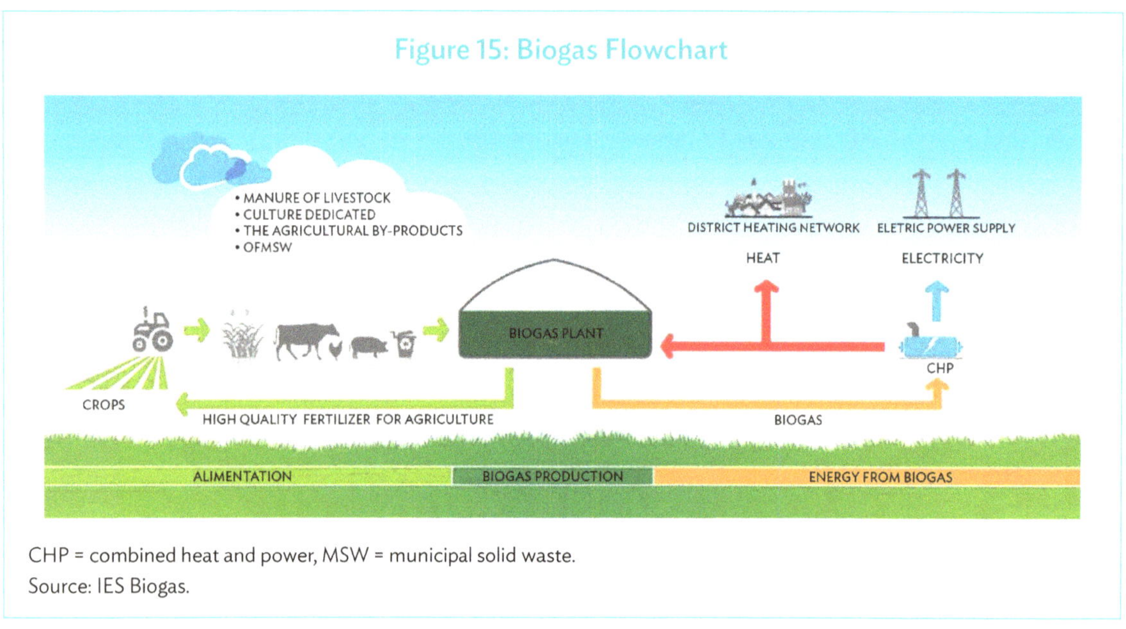

CHP = combined heat and power, MSW = municipal solid waste.
Source: IES Biogas.

Figure 16: Plant Layout

Source: IES Biogas.

Figure 17: Key Parameters in Design

❯	Feedstock availability and control	control of the substances to be used
❯	Conservative design	it has to be operated smoothly and simple
❯	Retention time	stable process
❯	Quality of the construction	reliability of the system
❯	Automation	high grade of automation and safety
❯	Biological and process know-how	optimized micronutrients can improve the process

Source: IES Biogas.

Table 9: Mass Balance

Mass Balance		Daily Quantity	Dry Substance (%DS)	Organic Dry Substance (%ODS)	Biogas Yield (Nm³/ton)
Input	Chicken manure	19.9 t/d	65.7	85.0	500
	Water	55.5 m³/day	—	—	—
Output from digesters	Digestate	68.5 m³/day	9.0	—	—
	Solid fraction of digestate	17.6 t/d	22.0	—	—
	Liquid fraction of digestate	50.9 m³/day	4.5	—	—
	Biogas	5,571 Nm³/d	—	—	—

— = negligible, DS = dry substance, ODS = organic dry substance, m³ = cubic meter, Nm³ = normal cubic meter, t/d = tons/day.
Source: IES Biogas.

Table 10: Energy Balance

Biogas Flow	5,571 Nm³/d
Methane content	58.0%
Methane flow	3,237 Nm³/d
Heat of combustion	10 kWh/ Nm³/d
Primary energy	32,370 kWh/d
Daily hours of operation	24 h
Gross electric power production (%)	540 kW

d = day, h = hour, kW = kilowatt, kWh = kilowatt-hour, m³ = cubic meter, Nm³ = normal cubic meter.
Source: IES Biogas.

BUSINESS MODEL

The following model has some assumptions and conservative grade (Table 11):

(i)   The power installed could be increased 10%–20% with substantially unchanged total project cost by using additional biomass (i.e., rice straw).

(ii)   The operating hours can reach 96% (IES Biogas average upon more than 80 biogas plants in operation worldwide).

(iii)   The cost of electricity might be higher depending on the region.

(iv)   No revenues have been computed for the heat, which could be used for the farm operation with additional saving on use of diesel.

(v)   The value of soil conditioner is assumed equal to the current value of chicken manure sold for fertilizing purposes. The real value should be much higher.

(vi)   The liquid foliar fertilizer is assumed as a cost related to the logistic of its spreading. It could be considered an additional revenue as common practice in Europe.

(vii)   The model is based on 92% plant availability average of the supplier.

(viii) It has been considered ₱7.50/kWh, which is the actual cost of electricity for the farm.

(ix)   The costs increase at 1.5% per year rate.

(x)   Minimal revenues have been considered for the selling of solid fertilizer after the process.

(xi)   The liquid fraction after separation will spread on rice fields as foliar fertilizer. Logistic cost has been calculated.

(xii)   A parasitic load of 8% of the generated energy has been calculated.

Table 11: Economic Analysis of the Biogas Project

HighCrest					
In green the parameters to be changed					
DATA			EUR–PHP		
Number of engines	1		exchange rate	55.51	
Power (kW)	600		USD–PHP		
Total installed power (kW)	600		exchange rate	50.69	
Operating hours	8,059				
Power generation factor	92.0%				
kWh produced per year	4,835,520				
REVENUES					
Energy Cost	€ 0.135	₱7.50	$0.15		
Electricity revenues	€ 653,331	₱36,266,400	$715,454.72		
Heat generation (kWh) (hot water 90 degrees)	4,835,520		$-		
Heat revenues	€ 0	₱ -	$-		
Solid fertilizer (tons/year)	6,400		$-	17.5	t/d
Value fertilizer/ton	€ 9.0	₱500.00	$9.86	351	bags/day
Revenues fertilizer	€ 57,647	₱3,200,000	$63,128.82		
TOTAL REVENUES	**€ 710,978**	**₱39,466,400**	**$778,583.55**		
COSTS					
Feeding Plan					
	ton/year	euro/ton	php/ton	total EUR	total php
Chicken manure	7,300	€ 0.00	₱ -	€ 0	₱ -
Water	0		₱ -		
Total feeding	7,300			€ 0	₱ -
Operation					
1 Supervisor/plant manager	€ 5,854.80	₱325,000.00	$6,411.52		
5 operators	€ 21,077.28	₱1,170,000.00	$23,081.48		
3 security	€ 9,133.49	₱507,000.00	$10,001.97		
1 accountant	€ 4,683.84	₱260,000.00	$5,129.22		
TOTAL COST OPERATION	€ 40,749.41	₱2,262,000.00	$44,624.19		

continued on next page

Table 11   *continued*

Maintenance					
Full service maintenance engine/kWh	€0.0100	₱0.56	€48,355	₱2,684,197.15	$52,953.19
Full service maintenance BGP/kWh	0.0050	₱0.28	€24,178	₱1,342,098.58	$26,476.59
Biological service/year + contingencies			€15,000	₱832,650.00	$16,426.32
TOTAL COST MAINTENANCE			€87,532.80	₱4,858,945.73	$95,856.10
Treatment Liquid Residue					
Liquid residue (m³/year)	18,500				
Cost of spreading/m³	€ 2.70	₱150.00	$2.96		
TOTAL COST TREATMENT	€ 49,990.99	₱2,775,000.00	$54,744.53		
Energy cost BGP (parasitic load)					
Parasitic load and losses	8%				
kWh	386,842				
Cost of kWh	€ 0.135	₱7.50	$0.15		
Energy cost	€ 52,266.5	₱2,901,312.00	$57,236.38		
Miscellaneous/ contingencies	€ 36,029.54	₱2,000,000.00	$39,455.51		
TOTAL O&M (OPEX)	**€ 266,569.23**	**PHP 14,797,257.73**	**$291,916.70**		
Generation Cost/kWh					
€ 0.055	₱3.06	$0.060			
EBITDA	**€ 444,409**	**PHP 24,669,142**	**$486,666.84**		
Investment costs					
TOTAL PROJECT COST (CAPEX)	**€ 3,185,012**	**PHP 176,800,000**	**$3,487,867.43**		
Payback time (years)	7.2				
Project IRR	11.2%				
Taxes	10%				

BGP = biogas to power; CAPEX = capital expenditure; d = day; EUR = euro; EBITDA = earnings before interest, tax, and depreciation, and amortization; IRR = internal rate of return; kW = kilowatt; kWh = kilowatt-hour; m³ = cubic meter; OPEX = operating expense; O&M = operation and maintenance; PHP = Philippine peso; USD = United States dollar; T = ton.

Source: IES Biogas.

FINANCING STRUCTURE

In most cases, the farm owner cannot to provide enough equity to finance the project. As well, major local banks are not inclined to proceed with project financing scheme due to a lack of knowledge of the technology. The project has been financed using a commercial loan with 70/30 leverage.

RESULTS

Producing biogas means:

> Production of renewable energy in the form of electrical and thermal energy

> Valorization of the biomass with the guarantee of a complementary income

> Reduction of the environmental impact of wastes thanks to their proper disposal

> Production of fertilizer with high organic and nutritive content for the soil

LESSONS

A relatively small biogas project guarantees easy and fast implementation. The target of the proposed project are the broiler farms of similar size in the Philippines. With the support of local cooperatives and poultry farmers associations, this model can serve as a standard solution to meet the environmental and energy challenges of the poultry industry.

THE DEVELOPER

IES BIOGAS, *an SNAM company*, is an Italian-based company leader in biogas plants and renewable energies.

The group was created and set up starting from the idea that the world's change cannot be stopped, but only analyzed and transformed into new opportunities. Thanks to its dynamism, along with over 10 years market experience, IES has enlarged its field of business and technical know-how, expanding its international presence. IES invests in renewable energy solutions and circular green economy offering complete and technically advanced plants at a worldwide level.

IES ENERGY GROUP specializes in the design, supply, construction, management and maintenance of renewable energy power plants, and waste-to-energy plants.

With more than 220 plants built in the last 10 years with 98.6% average efficiency, IES is the market leader in Europe for biogas plants construction. During the past years, IES has gone through an internationalization process and it is currently building and operating plants in South America, Republic of Korea, Indonesia, and the Philippines.

KEYWORDS

Biogas, anaerobic digestion, broiler manure, waste-to-energy, WtE

FURTHER READING

Poultry Manual. *Poultry Industry in the Philippines.* https://poultrymanual.com/2018/01/20/poultry-industry-philippines/

IES Biogas. www.iesbiogas.it.

Cargill. *Jollibee and Cargill inaugurate largest poultry processing plant in the Philippines.* https://www.cargill.com/2017/jollibee-and-cargill-inaugurate-largest-poultry-processing-plant.

1.7   Decentralized Waste Management Model

CONTEXT

Bengaluru (Bangalore) in India generates over 500 tons of solid waste daily. India enacted the Solid Waste Management Rules 2016, Plastic Waste Management Rules 2016, and E-Waste (Management) Rules 2016. These rules focus on decentralized systems to enable maximum recovery of waste. However, these rules face challenges in implementation due to lack of sound waste handling and management systems. Most of the municipal waste ends up either being burned or dumped in the open, water bodies, and landfills, further resulting in air, water, and soil pollution.

SOLUTION

To address these shortcomings, Saahas Zero Waste (SZW) adopts the principles of circular economy to reduce the consumption of resources and to recover resources from wastes generated by existing systems (Figure 28). SZW supports its customers' compliance to the relevant waste regulations through decentralized waste systems.

PROJECT SUMMARY

PROJECT NAME:
Decentralized Waste Management Model

CAPITAL COST:
$80,000

DEVELOPER:
Saahas Zero Waste

PROJECT HOST:
Saahas Zero Waste

GEOGRAPHICAL LOCATION:
Bangalore, Chennai, Goa, and Hyderabad, India

TYPE OF ENERGY PROJECT:
Circular economy

PROJECT COMPLETION YEAR:
2020

SZW has been able to achieve close to 90% of resource recovery from municipal waste through close management at source of generation, creation of higher value through the reduction in contamination of recyclable items, and engagement with the waste generators.

SZW delivers services around three verticals (Figure 29).

The SZW's Zero Waste Program helps its clients to become zero waste entities with emphasis on segregation at source: SZW operates on-site solutions for bulk waste generators including technology parks, educational institutions, and residential complexes. For smaller waste generators that may not have enough space, SZW offers holistic waste management including collection and processing of waste at its community waste centers, Kasa Rasas.

SZW also has an extended producer responsibility (EPR) program. SZW partners with packaging companies and electronic waste or e-waste producers to develop and implement a reverse logistics mechanism that facilitates in bringing back large volumes of post-consumption waste into the recycling chain.

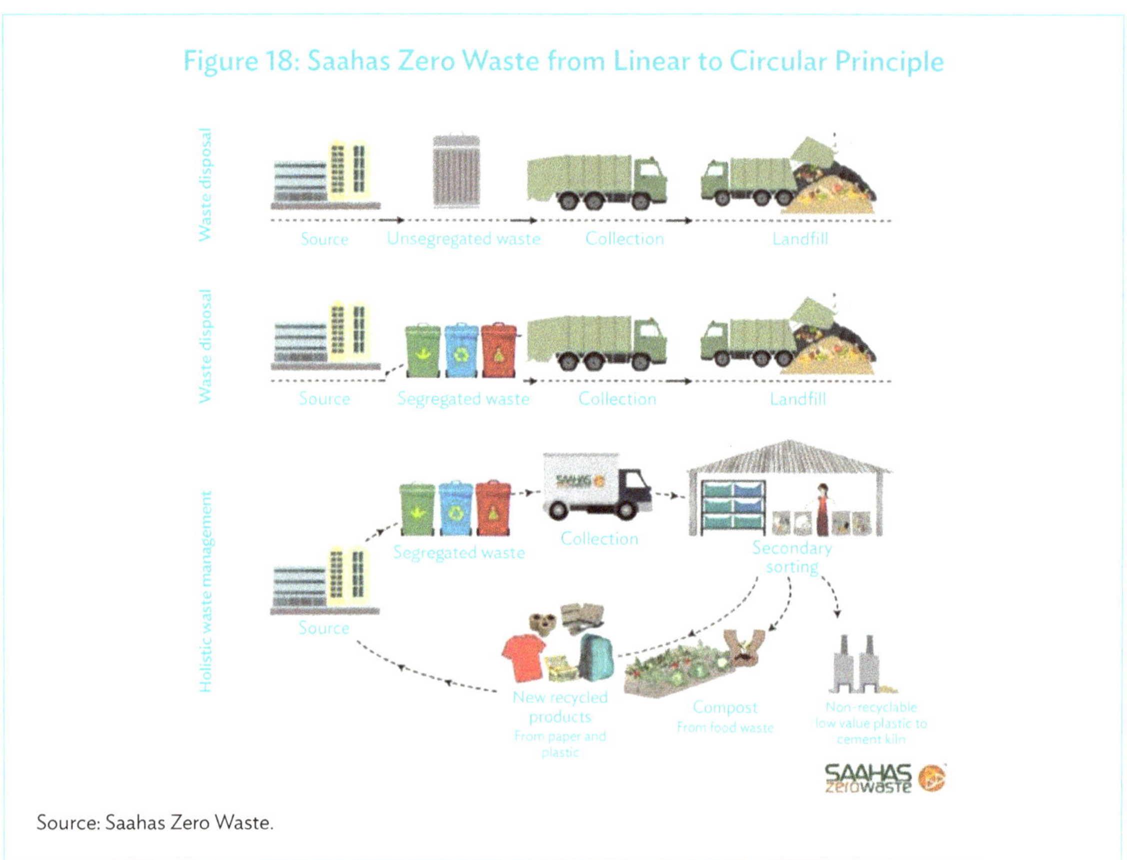

Source: Saahas Zero Waste.

As a part of the 'closing the loop' initiative, SZW offers products made from waste, including compost and a range of other recycled products like roofing sheets, chipboards, and stationary items. SZW also works with various women's self-help groups to upcycle textile waste into new products.

Zero Waste Program

As part of the zero waste program (ZWP), SZW has embedded waste management units within their customers' premises to manage the wet and dry waste. The wet waste is composted on-site and the dry waste goes through a preliminary secondary sorting exercise. In some situations, SZW composts some fractions of the wet waste on-site and takes the remaining to its off-site partner location where it is fed into a biogas digester. The gas is then bottled and sold to kitchens for cooking purposes. The compost on the other hand is used by the premises for its landscaping. All dry waste is transported to SZW's material recovery facility (MRF) for further segregation, aggregation, compaction, and dispatch to appropriate recycling facilities and co-processing units such as cement kilns.

Given that the segregation at source is the bedrock for maximum recovery of resources, it continuously engages with the waste generators to increase awareness and change behavior toward segregation and holistic waste management.

More than 50% of SZW's staff are women. SZW uses a management information system (MIS) called Zoho to capture and analyze data on collection, transportation, and processing of waste.

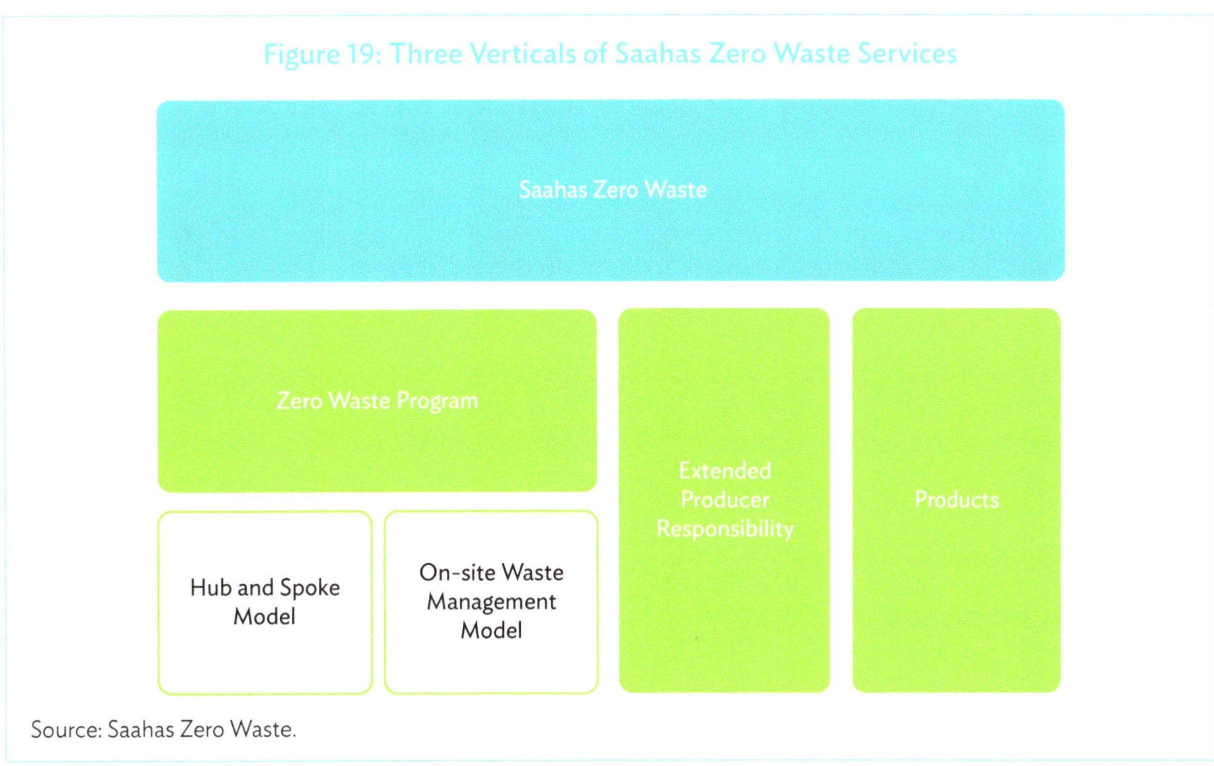

Source: Saahas Zero Waste.

Extended Producer Responsibility Program

India has framed laws for extended producer responsibility (EPR) for plastic waste and e-waste. SZW assists manufacturers and brand owners of electronic goods and plastic packaging in reverse logistics of post-consumer plastic waste and e-waste to ensure environmentally sound management of such waste.

Multinational companies whose operations generate plastic packaging waste or e-waste are required to comply with these newly framed regulations. SZW partners with local aggregators, waste picker colonies, and the informal waste sector for collection of different streams of plastic waste including low-grade plastics, multilayered plastics, high-density polyethylene (HDPE), low-density polyethylene, etc., and e-waste as required by its clients. These wastes thereafter sent to third party authorized end destinations such as recycling units and co-processing plants for safe processing and disposal. As a part of working with the informal sector, SZW also integrates and upgrades different stakeholders into formal industry and systems. In addition, SZW's MIS system enables capturing of data and preparing detailed reports for its customers to use for regulation compliance and impact measurement.

Products

To close the loop on waste management and recovery, SZW collaborates with third-party vendors to manufacture products out of different waste streams such as paper, Tetra Pak, aluminum, PET bottles, and plastic. Its current products portfolio includes stationery, chipboards, roofing sheets, and apparel that are sold to various types of end-customers including corporates, educational institutions, and individuals. SZW also works with brands and organizations for ethical sourcing of pre- and/or post-consumer textile waste and local self-help groups to convert textile waste into second life or zero waste products.

TECHNOLOGY

SZW maintains an MRF and adopts a data management system in operating its business.

Material Recovery Facility

The MRF involves different processes and each process uses several tools and equipment to optimize the efficiency and promote ideal ergonomic working conditions of the staff.

The incoming materials are segregated to enable the various waste streams to be separated from each other to ensure that each stream reaches its appropriate destination. The conveyor defines the rate at which segregation occurs in the MRF. The conveyor moves the material from the ground floor to the elevated platform on which segregation is carried out (Figure 30). The material once sorted out into several categories are either collected in bags or dropped in the bays that are located underneath the elevated platform (Figure 31). The material to be dropped in the bays are decided based on the percentage composition of incoming waste by weight. The sorted materials are compressed through bailing to optimize storage and transportation. The most commonly used baler at the MRF is hydraulically operated and loaded manually. It takes about 20 to 30 minutes to create one bale depending on the material type due to the time taken to bring the aggregated material. Figure 32 shows the staff by the baler.

The movement of material is a crucial factor in determining the overall workforce required while the storage facility determines the space required by an MRF. The hand-operated truck is currently used to move the incoming material (in bags) to the incoming material storage area and a semi-electric stacker

Material Loading onto the Conveyor. The conveyor moves the material from the ground floor to the elevated platform on which segregation is carried out (photo by Saahas Zero Waste).

Staff Segregating Waste. The sorted materials are compressed through bailing to optimize storage and transportation (photo by Saahas Zero Waste).

Staff by the Baler. The most commonly used baler at the material recovery facility is hydraulically operated and loaded manually (photo by Saahas Zero Waste).

is used to move the bales from the baler to outgoing material storage area and then to the unloading bay. SZW is planning to acquire new equipment to improve the current operation efficiency.

SZW adopts data management system in its business, allowing the practice of reduce, reuse, and recycle, and to better understand the generator (source) and composition of the waste qualitatively and quantitatively. The quantitative data is obtained by segregating each stream of waste and measuring their quantities. The segregation categories (streams) are chosen carefully based on the chemical composition and recyclability of the material. Data collection happens at multiple points and for different reasons in the waste management process. While data collection at certain points enables optimization of the process, at other points it acts as indicators to take actionable feedback to eliminate or reduce certain types of materials.

With effective Internet of Things or IOT devices, the data accuracy can be increased multi-fold. There is up to a 20% difference in the data collected at MRF through weighment slips and data uploaded manually into Zoho ERP from on-site locations. This can be avoided by relevant IOT-enabled smart devices to collect data at every checkpoint.

BUSINESS MODEL

The business model has two sources of revenue: a service fee and revenues from waste. Table 12 summarizes the source of cost and revenue of the SZW three business verticals.

Table 12: Revenue and Costs of Saahas Zero Waste Three Verticals

Biomass Verticals	Revenue			Costs	
ZWP	Service fees from generators	Scrap sale to recycler	Direct-labor/ Transport/ consumables	Co-processing cost	Indirect-coordination/ Admin/Rent
EPR	Service fees from producer	Scrap sale to recycler	Material purchase from informal sector/ source / transport	Co-processing cost	Indirect-coordination/ Admin
Recycled products	Sale price		Manufacture costs/ transport costs		Indirect-Coordination/ Admin

EPR = extended producer responsibility, ZWP = zero waste program.
Source: Saahas Zero Waste.

Operating a 10 TPD decentralized plant managing dry waste such as SZW's MRF requires a facility with 10,000 square feet, with construction and equipment cost being approximately $217,000. The operational cost (including processing waste at the facilities and sending the recyclable waste to recyclers, excluding cost of collection and transportation from source) is approximately $950/TPD (i.e., 10 metric ton [Mt]/day). The revenue streams of SZW include service fee, which is $26 processing 1 ton of dry waste and sale of high-value recyclables (processed waste) at $90/ton.

Table 13 summarizes the financials of SZW's ZWP, which also includes management of biodegradable waste. When waste is processed at source where cost is minimized, at the same time, reducing or eliminating collection/transportation cost, it can generate net revenue of around $1.34 million per year when managing approximately 32 Mt of waste.

Table 13: Financials of Zero Waste Program

Item	Waste Management Services	Waste Sales	Operational Expenses	Total ($)
Unit price ($/ton)	145	94.0	119	
Operational daily capacity (ton)	25	7.5		
Total daily revenue ($)	3,592	715.3	3,842	
Total yearly revenue ($)				1,343,864
Number of operation days (yearly): 312 $1:INR75				

INR = Indian rupees.
Source: Saahas Zero Waste.

FINANCING STRUCTURE

SZW received approximately $1.15 million funding from social impact investors in India who currently hold 40% share of the company. It currently has 250 employees managing 75 tons of waste per day across Bangalore, Chennai, Goa, and Hyderabad, and other cities in India. SZW supports the livelihood at the base of the pyramid for its field staff with emphasis on health and safety. By March 2020, the company has reached its breakeven point.

RESULTS

Social Impact

Majority of the waste management industry in India continues to be informal and the waste collectors are typically daily wage contract workers who work long hours without any protective equipment, and are paid far less than the minimum wages and statutory benefits. The waste pickers in India are also predominantly women and children, who are also most susceptible to exploitation from several fronts. Unlike majority of these players in the waste sector, all SZW's 250 employees (including the field staff that handle and manage waste at client locations) are permanent staff and more than 50% of them are women who belong to the base of the economic pyramid. They are paid in accordance with law and provided with all social security benefits that are mandated by law. The staff are required to wear personal protective equipment whenever they are handling waste and they are regularly provided with training on health and safety. Having permanent staff on its payroll ensures also that SZW has complete visibility over payment of wages and social security benefits and their health and safety are ensured. This results in creating dignified, sustainable, and safe livelihoods for one of the most disadvantaged sections of the society. As per the social impact survey carried out by one of SZW's investors, employees have had several benefits after joining SZW such as (i) lower poverty likelihood, (ii) increased ability to save and repay their existing debts, (iii) increase household income by 105% on average, and (iv) increased employees' ability to buy both utility and productive assets that have improved their quality of life.

Environmental Impact

SZW manages over 75 tons of waste every day and it has zero tolerance toward dumping or burning of waste in the open. Each stream of waste that is collected is sent to an appropriate end destination where it is either composted, bio-methanized, recycled, co-processed, or landfilled. The environmental impact of SZW operation is based on the amount of waste reduced, the number of tons of waste managed per day and diverted from landfills, public spaces, and water bodies. In addition, scientific management of waste also results in reduction in emission of greenhouse and noxious gases, which consequently reduces the overall carbon footprint. Over the financial year ended 31 March 2020, SZW has managed over 20,000 tons of solid waste and e-waste through composting, bio-methanation, recycling, and co-processing, thereby reducing annual GHG emissions by approximately 56,971 metric tons of carbon dioxide emissions (MT CO_2e). Its calculations are based on the Greenhouse Gas Equivalencies Calculator created by the US Environmental Protection Agency (https://www.epa.gov/energy/greenhouse-gas-equivalencies-calculator) for voluntarily reporting of GHG emissions reductions from several different waste management practices. In addition, it has been able to successfully reduce the use of disposable/one-time used items (such as paper cups, cutlery, and plastic bags) with most of SZW's institutional customers. This has resulted in reducing carbon emissions during manufacture, transportation, and disposal of these products. Further, by creating a retail market for products made out of waste, it reduces the demand for virgin material, thereby reducing extraction of natural resources from our planet.

Economic Impact

Given that SZW's business model has proved to be financially viable, it is leading the way for other formal players to enter the sector, thereby formalizing the waste management industry. It also works with recyclers, bio-methanation units, co-processors, and other end destinations that contribute toward an economy that is based on waste management and the resources recovered from waste. In addition, for its EPR program, SZW works with the informal sector on a micro-entrepreneur model where it partners with players in the informal sector and purchases the wastes they collect at fair rates. However, to partner with SZW, the informal player needs to comply with minimum standards of health, safety, and environmental protection, and ensure that no child labor is used in its operations. Further, all transactions between SZW and the informal players happen through normal banking channels and there are no cash transactions. These lead to formalization of the waste industry, which in turn results in (i) implementation of safety standards and compliance with law, (ii) reduction in exploitation of certain disadvantageous sections of the society, and (iii) contribution to the economy and revenues of the state.

Health Impact

The United States (US) Public Health Service has identified 22 human diseases that are linked to improper solid waste management. Given that SZW currently manages waste every day on a scientific basis, its operations have an impact on the health of local populations especially those that are most susceptible in the event of an outbreak of diseases due to poor waste management. SZW plans to increasingly work with various governmental authorities to implement sustainable waste management solutions within their respective jurisdictions. This will enable to impact the quality of life of more and more people who are currently plagued by the waste management crisis in India.

THE DEVELOPER

Saahas Zero Waste (SZW) is a socioenvironmental enterprise that believes in a circular economy, where all waste is converted to resources. Registered in 2013, SZW is recognized as a start-up by the Department of Industrial Policy and Promotion, Government of India.

KEYWORDS

Saahas Zero Waste, circular economy, solid waste, extended product responsibility, Zero Waste Program, material recovery facility, inclusive business, sustainability, holistic waste management, resource recovery, waste hierarchy, 4R principle of waste, plastic waste, e-waste.

1.8   Carbon Masters Koramangala Plant

CONTEXT

In a world with 7.6 billion people, over 50% of the population reside in urban areas, which is further set to rise over the coming decades (75% by 2040). The rapid pace of urbanization has the potential to bring about great changes for the betterment of the society but also presents many environmental challenges.

Globally, 11.2 billion tons of waste is generated every year and the amount of waste is among the biggest threats affecting our ecosystem. Solid waste dumped at landfill sites produce large amounts of methane, which accounts for 12% percent of total global emissions.

Methane is the second most common GHG after carbon dioxide and has 32 times the global warming potential of carbon dioxide. In India, out of the 62 million tons of waste generated across 4,000 cities and towns, 50% percent is organic and biodegradable, which can be disposed in environmentally friendly methods.

PROJECT SUMMARY

PROJECT NAME:
Carbon Masters Koramangala plant

CAPITAL COST:
$473,050 (₹33 million)

DEVELOPER:
Carbon Masters India Private Ltd.

PROJECT HOST:
Carbon Masters India Private Ltd.

GEOGRAPHICAL LOCATION:
Bangalore, India

TYPE OF ENERGY PROJECT:
Biogas from waste

PROJECT COMPLETION YEAR:
2018

SOLUTION

Carbon Masters India Private Limited has devised an innovative way for managing the organic waste by collecting and converting the waste into useful fuel and fertilizer. Carbon Masters collects the waste generated in their bio-compressed natural gas (CNG) trucks from various bulk waste-generating establishments such as IT parks, residential complexes, and restaurants, and then treats the waste anaerobically to produce biogas and organic slurry. The gas is purified, compressed, and bottled to form Carbonlites, while the slurry is treated to produce Carbonlites organic manure. Carbon Masters also builds distributed container size biogas generator system directly supplying gas to nearby restaurants by feeding the food or organic waste from the restaurant.

TECHNOLOGY

Biogas typically refers to a gas produced by the biological breakdown of organic matter in the absence of oxygen. The gas mainly comprises of methane (CH_4) and carbon dioxide (CO_2). The feedstock for biogas production includes agricultural waste, food waste, vegetable waste, horticulture waste, animal waste, kitchen waste, and so on. The gas is generated through a process called anaerobic digestion, an action that is facilitated by various groups of anaerobic bacteria. Biogas plants in India are traditionally built as a civil construction with a circular design for the anaerobic digester. Bio-CNG is the result of purifying this biogas to >90% methane and compressing it in cylinders. Table 14 provides information on biogas composition. Carbon Masters has also developed an anaerobic digester housed within a refurbished shipping container (Figure 33), which is ideal for on-site WtE conversion in cities where space is a consideration (It occupies one-third of the space of a conventional anaerobic digester). Carbonlites purification unit and bottling is shown in Figure 34.

Carbonlites in a Box: Carbon Masters' Container-Size Digester. The Carbonlites in a Box is ideal for on-site waste-to-energy conversion in cities where space is a consideration (photo by Carbon Masters India Private Ltd.).

Table 14: Biogas Composition

Components	Symbol	Biogas (%)	Bio-CNG
Methane	CH_4	50–60	> 90%
Carbon dioxide	CO_2	45–48	< 4 %
Hydrogen sulfide	H_2S	< 0.1	< 20 ppm

CNG = compressed natural gas, ppm = parts per million.
Source: Carbon Masters India Private Ltd.

Carbon Masters has developed its own innovative gas storage technologies –Cylinders and Cascades. Figure 35 shows carbonlites cylinders—process flow as the following:

(i)   Cascades to hold two to four cylinders with capacities ranging from 19 kilograms (kgs) to 30 kgs.

(ii) A pressure-reducing system is used to reduce the pressure from 150 bar to 20 bar and then to 2 bar before being piped into the kitchen. Minimal modification is done to burners to work with Carbonlites.

(iii) Carbonlites Cylinders are transported to client location daily as per requirements via a bio-CNG truck.

(iv) Empty cylinders are collected daily and transported back to Carbon Masters biogas plants.

(v) The gas is piped from the cylinders to the kitchen and can be substituted for LPG and utilized for cooking.

The by-product of the biogas production is high-quality, carbon-enriched organic manure (Figure 36). The indiscriminate use of chemical fertilizers in India over many years and the lack of the addition of organic material has contributed to soils lacking in useful micronutrients, particularly carbon, which are vital in maintaining healthy fertile soils. An increasing number of farmers are recognizing this and are moving to organic farming or seeking to reduce their dependence on chemical fertilizers and pesticides.

Carbonlites Purification Unit and Bottling. Carbonlites cylinders are transported to client location daily or as per requirements via a bio-CNG truck (photo by Carbon Masters India Private Ltd.).

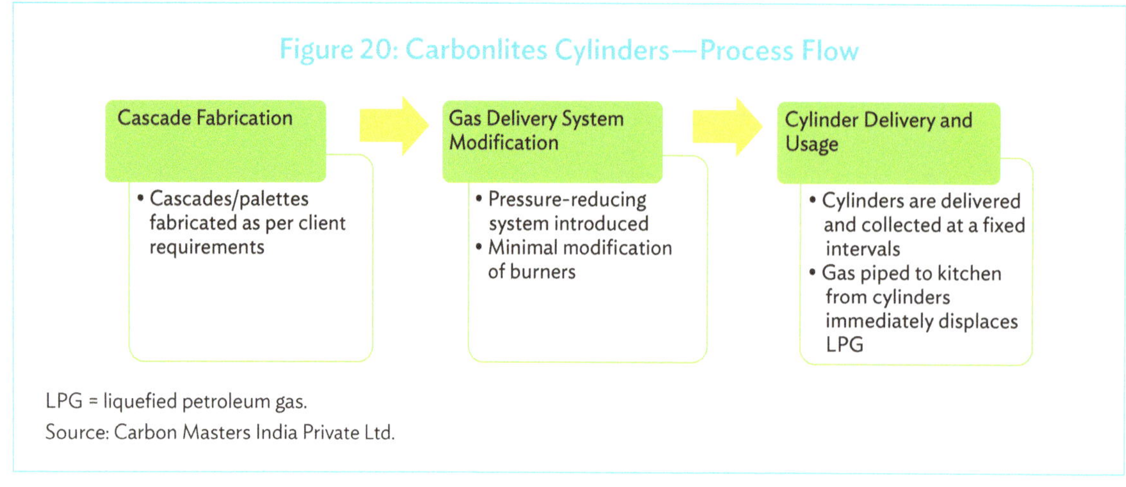

LPG = liquefied petroleum gas.
Source: Carbon Masters India Private Ltd.

High-Quality Carbonlites Organic Manure. This carbon-enriched organic manure can return useful micronutrients to the soil, improving soil health and fertility (photo by Carbon Masters India Private Ltd.).

One of the identified barriers to this is the lack of good quality organic manure, a gap Carbonlites organic manure seeks to fill.

It is made by combining the digestate from the anaerobic digestion process with biomass via a windrow composting process where the digestate is mixed with garden leaves and wood (branches, twigs) in a particular ratio of greens and brows to form a compost. It is then put through a sieving process to create Carbonlites organic manure. This carbon-enriched organic manure can return useful micronutrients to the soil, improving soil health and fertility. Carbon Masters has also developed an additional bio-enriched version of the product by adding a bio-fertilizer inoculant. This bio- fertilizer inoculant increases the nitrogen fixing in the soil enhancing the performance of the manure, making it particularly useful for fully organic farmers who do not want to use chemical fertilizers to fix nitrogen in the soil.

BUSINESS MODEL

The Carbon Masters business model facilitates a circular economy through which waste is converted into Carbonlites: Bio-CNG and organic fertilizer. This solves the problem of managing waste in cities, displaces fossil fuels, and chemical fertilizers. See Figure 37 for its business model illustration.

Carbonlites Bottled Bio-CNG is used as a substitute to LPG for cooking. Right from collection of segregated waste until the production of Carbonlites and organic manure, Carbon Masters, adopting a 360-degree approach, ensures that it manages organic waste, and produces and consumes clean fuel. By handling the operation and maintenance and sale of the products, Carbon Masters has created a sustainable revenue sharing model, thus creating a circular economy.

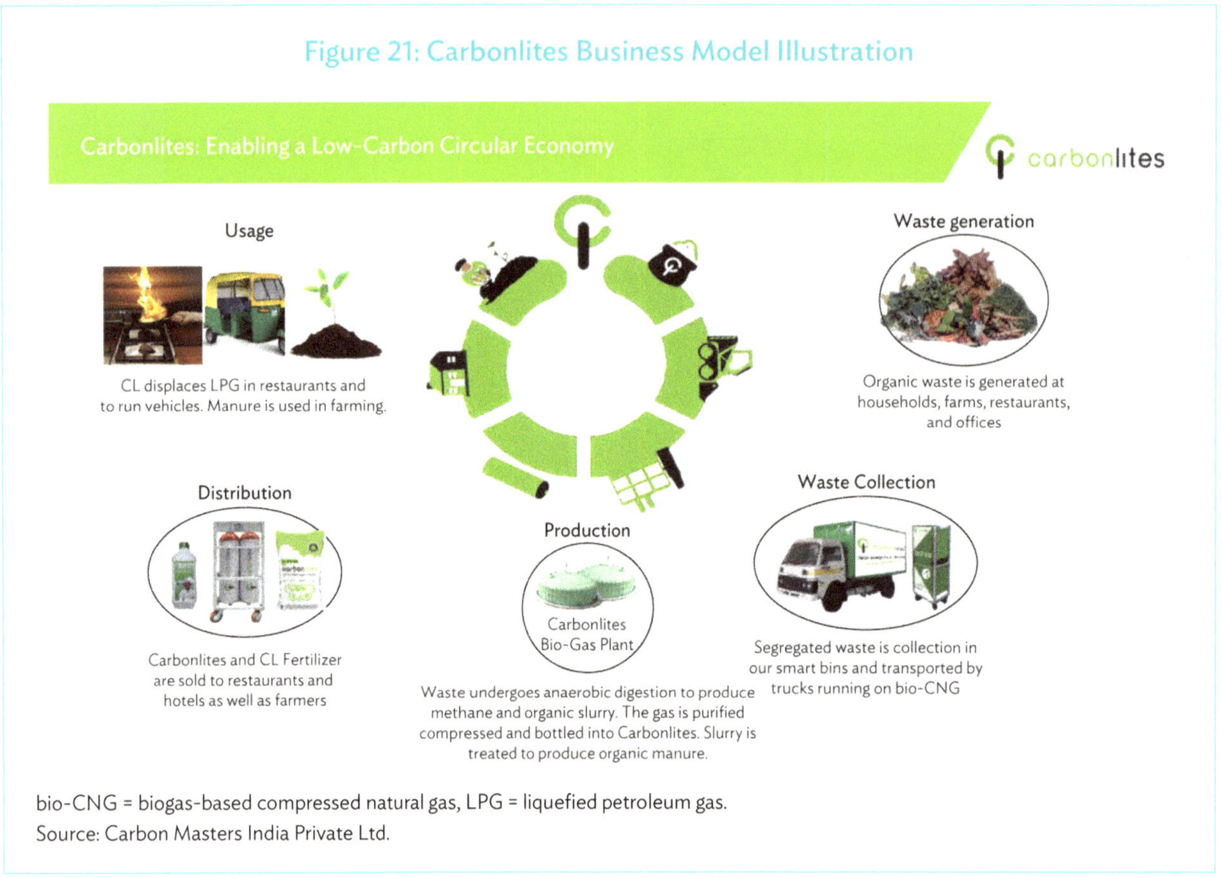

bio-CNG = biogas-based compressed natural gas, LPG = liquefied petroleum gas.
Source: Carbon Masters India Private Ltd.

FINANCING STRUCTURE

Table 15 summarizes the amount of waste Carbon Masters collected per day and year from one their facilities, which has to capacity to process 10 TPD of organic waste, and consequently the amount of bio-CNG and organic fertilizer produced and carbon emissions saved (Table 16).

Table 15: Costs and Revenue of Carbon Masters Waste-to-Energy Facility

Revenue Generation[3]	First Phase	Equivalent ($)
Waste input	10 tons	
Gas sales/day (in kgs) (after captive consumption)	300	
Price per kg	INR75.00	1.08
Organic fertilizer generation (tons per day)	1	
CM selling price of organic fertilizer (per ton)	INR8,000	
Gas revenue per day	INR22,500	322.53
Organic fertilizer revenue per day	INR8,000	114.68

continued on next page

4    $1:INR69.76 as of 31 December 2018 (https://forex.adb.org/fx_rate/getRates).

Table 15   *continued*

Revenue Generation[3]	First Phase	Equivalent ($)
Total revenue per day	INR30,500	437.21
Total revenue per month (INR)	INR927,708	13,298.57
Total revenue per year (INR)	INR11,132,500	159,582.85
PRODUCTION COST		
Operation cost per month (INR)	INR250,000	3,583.71
Operation cost per month (INR)	INR250,000	3,583.71
Profit per month (INR)	INR677,708	9,714.85
Profit per year (INR)	INR8,132,500	116,578.26
Capital Costs (INR)		
CAPEX for 10 TPD (INR)	INR33,000,000	473,050.45
Simple payback (Years)	4.1 Years	

CAPEX = capital expenditure, CM = Carbon Masters, INR = Indian rupee, kg = kilogram, TPD - tons per day.
Source: Carbon Masters India Private Ltd.

Table 16: Amount of Waste Collected, Useful Products Generated, and Carbon Dioxide Saved

Waste Collected	Bio-CNG Produced	Organic Fertilizer Produced	Carbon Emissions Saved
10 tons per day	400 kgs per day	1 ton per day	12.9 tons CO_2e per day
3,650 tones/year	146 Tons/year	365 Tones/year	4700 Tons CO_2e Annually

CNG = compressed natural gas, CO_2e = carbon dioxide emissions.
Source: Carbon Masters India Private Ltd.

RESULTS

The waste collected, which otherwise would go to landfills, is converted into useful products:

Carbonlites Bio-CNG is bottled in unique cascades with two to four cylinders delivered via proprietary pressure-reducing systems providing a carbon-neutral gas to kitchens, boilers, or engines. Total in-use cost savings are 10%–15% when compared to LPG usage and far higher when replacing diesel.

Carbonlites organic manure is produced by combining the biogas slurry with garden waste (another pain point in cities, where the garden waste is burned for disposal). The fertilizer has been widely tested across Karnataka and gained approval from conventional and organic farmers alike. The benefits of this being the following:

(i)   Organic waste is diverted from landfills mitigating methane emissions.

(ii)   The LPG displaced in kitchens by Carbonlites results in carbon-neutral kitchens having a zero carbon footprint from their energy usage.

(iii) Diesel/petrol replaced in running trucks on Carbonlites reduces city pollution by reducing particulate matter and tackles climate change by reducing GHG emissions.

(iv)   At a ward level, less garbage is dumped in streets producing cleaner cities.

(v)   It creates new jobs in the otherwise informal waste management sector.

(vi)   Providing Carbonites organic manure reduces farmers' dependence on energy-intensive chemical fertilizers, further reducing GHG emissions both from the production of chemical fertilizers, and the NOx emissions at the farm level. It also and improves soil health by increasing the soil organic matter.

In October 2018, Carbonlites Initiative received the World Wildlife Fund or WWF Climate Solver award for GHG emission reduction efforts. WWF calculate the impact of Carbonlites, if scaled globally, will be 28 million tons of CO_2 reduction by 2027. A link to short documentary shot by WWF is given below:

https://www.youtube.com/watch?v=IK0I4reyKvg

LESSONS

One of the major reasons for failure of several biogas projects in India is that the people who build the plants do not operate it, and those who operate it are not involved in the sale of the output. Carbon Masters learned that it was imperative to be involved in all aspects of the project to understand the challenges involved to make the project feasible. It was observed that a combined heat and power (CHP) biogas project solution would not be economically feasible in the Indian market. A model that generates revenue from direct heating applications of purified biogas (transport, cooking, etc.) along with a secondary revenue stream from fertilizer products made from the digestate is required.

A conventional model for managing municipal wet waste involves the transport of the waste over long distances to a biogas plant located outside the city. With innovative solutions like Carbonlites in-a-box, Carbon Masters has been able to cut down the costs and turnaround time of small plants. This allows for a decentralized approach to waste processing, i.e., there can be several plug-and-play biogas plants within the city enabling localized circular economy zones.

THE DEVELOPER

Carbon Masters are the owners of the brand Carbonlites. Carbonlites is carbon mitigation in a bottle, a box, and a bag. It is India's first branded bottled bio-CNG and organic fertilizer product with proven applications for commercial cooking displacing LPG, as a transport fuel replacing diesel and petrol, for backup power generation, and displaces chemical fertilizers. It saves both costs and carbon emissions. It has a registered capital of $584,000 and has a board consisting of two co-founders, one independent director, and two investor directors. The shares of the company are currently held by co-founders (majority shares), VC firm Sangam Ventures, and IAN, the world's largest angel network group.

KEYWORDS

Carbonlites, Carbon Masters, Waste to Energy, bottled bio-CNG, biogas, organic manure, renewable energy, circular economy

FURTHER READING

Carbonlites. www.carbonlites.com

Carbonlites: *WWF Climate Solver 2017*. www.youtube.com/watch?v=IK0I4reyKvg.

Manupriya. 2018. All eyes on biogas plants as cities continue to grapple with overflowing landfills. *Citizen Matters*. 29 December. www.citizenmatters.in/biogas-plants-india-waste-management-source-segregation-9595.

DW. Bangalore startup turns garbage into gas. https://www.dw.com/en/bangalore-startup-turns-garbage-into-gas/a-51034766.

1.9   Combined Heat and Power Facility

CONTEXT

The project is in line with Pepsi Cola Products Philippines Inc. (PCPPI) program called POWERPLAY, which aims to reduce the cost of energy in the operation of its bottling plants. Pepsi Rosario, PCPPI's bottling plant in Rosario, La Union, utilized oil-fired boilers fueled by low sulfur fuel oil (LSFO), which is subject to price volatility and emits GHGs that contribute to global warming. The high cost of LSFO and electricity prompted PCPPI to look for alternative sources of energy such as biomass to meet the requirements of its plants. It signed a memorandum of understanding with Solutions Using Renewable Energy (SURE) Inc. to develop a renewable energy project that can reduce energy cost of Pepsi Rosario by at least 20%.

SOLUTION

The project was originally designed to include the installation of a 10-ton per hour (tph) high-pressure boiler that will supply the steam for a 1,250 kW turbine generator and 1-tph process steam for Pepsi's bottle washing. With parasitic load of 250 kW, the net power generation will be 1,000 kW. Pepsi's requirement is 650 kW average, the excess of 350 kW will be supplied to the local distribution utility under a power supply agreement. As the steam requirements of Pepsi increased to nearly 3 tph when it added a new bottling line, it was decided that a separate 3-tph process boiler would be installed.

Rice husk is the feedstock or fuel for the boilers. About 65–70 TPD is required. It will be sourced from the rice mills and rice husk traders in La Union and Pangasinan. Rosario, La Union is right in the boundary of Pangasinan province, the third-biggest producer of rice husk in the Philippines. The rice husk supply at the plant supply is shown in Figure 38.

<table>
<tr><td colspan="2">PROJECT SUMMARY</td></tr>
<tr><td>PROJECT NAME:</td><td></td></tr>
<tr><td colspan="2">Combined Heat and Power facility</td></tr>
<tr><td>CAPITAL COST:</td><td></td></tr>
<tr><td colspan="2">$5.8 million</td></tr>
<tr><td>DEVELOPER:</td><td></td></tr>
<tr><td colspan="2">SUREPEP, Inc.</td></tr>
<tr><td>PROJECT HOST:</td><td></td></tr>
<tr><td colspan="2">Pepsi Cola Products Philippines, Inc.</td></tr>
<tr><td>GEOGRAPHICAL LOCATION:</td><td></td></tr>
<tr><td colspan="2">Rosario, La Union, Philippines</td></tr>
<tr><td>TYPE OF ENERGY PROJECT:</td><td></td></tr>
<tr><td colspan="2">Combined Heat and Power</td></tr>
<tr><td>PROJECT COMPLETION YEAR:</td><td></td></tr>
<tr><td colspan="2">2015</td></tr>
</table>

Rice Husk Supply at Plant Site. About 65–70 tonnes per day of rice husk is required for the operation of combined heat and power facility in Rosario, La Union, Philippines (Source: SUREPEP, Inc.).

TECHNOLOGY

Following are the main technologies employed in the project:

(i) **High-pressure biomass broiler.** The rice husk undergoes combustion in the furnace of the boiler. Tubes within the boiler containing purified, de-aerated, and preheated water, are heated up to produce saturated steam. Before exiting the boiler, the saturated steam passes through the superheater where the water is vaporized into superheated steam, creating high pressure before it is directed to the steam turbine. The boiler capacity is 10 tph of steam with temperature of 420°C and pressure of 45 kg/cm^2.

(ii) **Steam turbine generator.** As the steam flows past the turbines spinning blades, the steam expands and cools. The potential energy of the steam is thus turned into kinetic energy in rotating the turbine's blades. Because steam turbines generate rotary motion, they are particularly suited for driving electrical generators for power generation. The turbine is connected to a generator with an axle, which in turn produces energy via a magnetic field that produces electric current. The steam turbine generator is rated 1,250 kW.

(iii) **Process boiler.** A process boiler is a low-pressure boiler. The one used in this project is rated 12 kg/cm^2 producing 3 tph of saturated steam at 190°C. The steam is piped to Pepsi Rosario's bottle-washing vessel to maintain the temperature of its washing solution at 70°C. The boiler also uses rice husk as fuel.

The process flow of Pepsi Rosario Biomass Power Plant is shown in Figure 39.

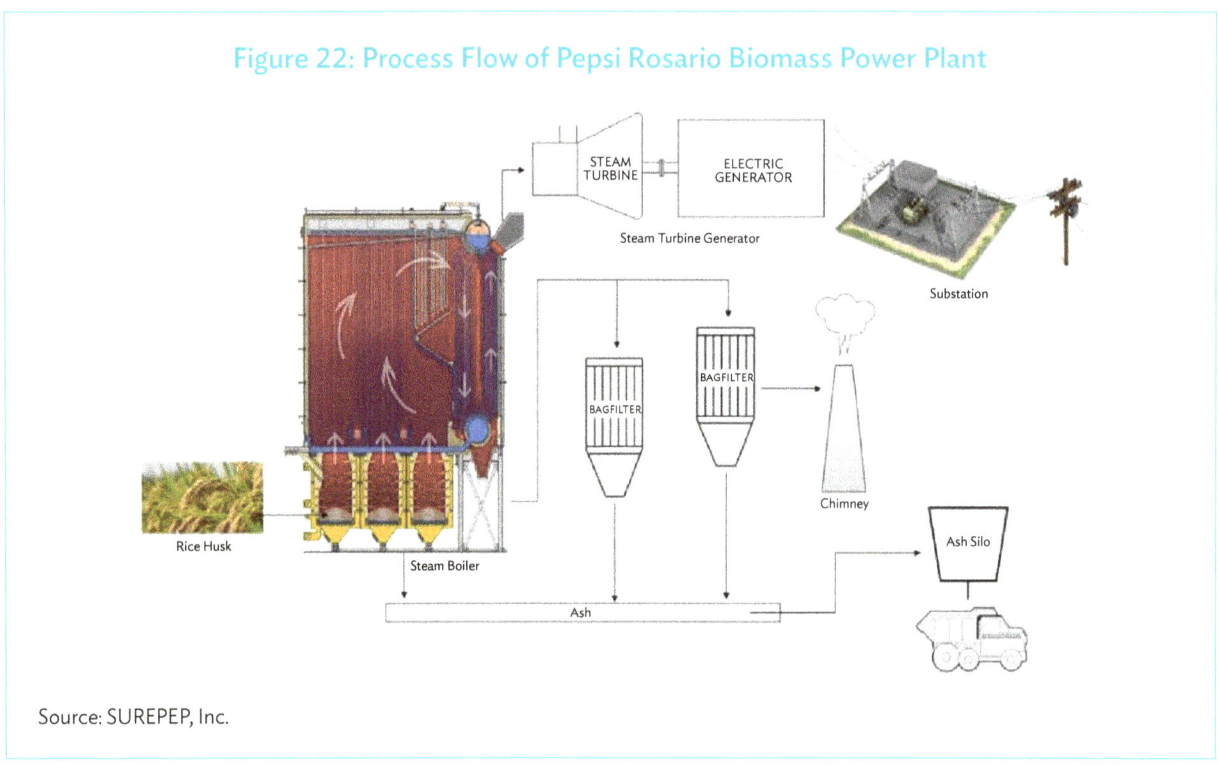

BUSINESS MODEL

SUREPEP was created to be the special purpose company to implement the project. The 10-year build-own-operate-supply-transfer agreement signed by SURE with PCPPI for the development of the biomass cogeneration facility for Pepsi's bottling plant in Rosario, La Union, Philippines was transferred to SUREPEP. As per the contract, SUREPEP will sell electricity and steam to Pepsi at 20% discount based on the current power utility rate and its computed cost of generating steam if it uses LSFO at current prices.

FINANCING STRUCTURE

The project entailed a total cost of $5.8 million. The project was financed through equity contribution of investors amounting to $3.8 million and the balance of $2 million was financed through a loan with interest rate of 7.5% payable in 5 years excluding a 2-year grace period.

RESULTS

About 2.5 tph of steam is being delivered to Pepsi or about 1.3 million kg/month. That is equivalent to savings of 100,000 liters of LSFO per month. However, power generation only lasted for a few months because of synchronizing problems with the distribution utility grid voltage being unstable. Later the turbine became defective and needed to be replaced. From a single-stage turbine, which will be replaced with a multistage turbine using the same boiler, the power generation can be increased to 2,000 kW. However, this will need additional investment, renegotiation of contracts, and renewal of licenses.

LESSONS

The problem with the grid voltage occurred during the construction of the project and was not anticipated during the design of the interconnection scheme, which resulted to synchronization problems. This was addressed by the distribution utility much later, and after the steam turbine became defective. This possible critical interconnection scenario should have been considered in the design even if it would have entailed additional cost.

THE DEVELOPER

SUREPEP is only a special purpose company. It is SURE that developed the project from inception to implementation. SURE is a developer of renewable energy projects in the Philippines with presence also in Singapore and Viet Nam. It is now more focused on conversion of MSW to other products such as electricity, biomethane, and fuel oil.

KEYWORDS

low sulfur fuel oil, combined heat and power, steam turbine generator, high pressure biomass boiler, process boiler, build-own-operate-supply transfer, SUREPEP

FURTHER READING

SURE, Inc. https://sureinc.wordpress.com/company/.

SURE, Inc. *Projects*. http://sureinc.wixsite.com/sure/projects.

1.10   150-Kilowatt Electrical Power Generation in Dual Fuel Mode

CONTEXT

The project host is a private rice mill located in the state of Uttar Pradesh, India. The rice mill was generating 168 tons of paddy per day.

As the rice industry was highly competitive, the rice mill owner aimed to increase its production while reducing operational costs. The area was experiencing severe power interruptions, thus the rice mill was dependent on 100% diesel, which was quite expensive. The rice mill wanted to generate electricity at lower cost using available resources as feedstock.

SOLUTION

There are many renewable energy options available such as solar, wind, hydro, and biomass. Wind and hydro are site specific, while the availability of solar and wind are intermittent. These renewable energy systems cannot be deployed to meet the captive power requirements of an industry operating for 16–24 hours per day such as this private rice mill.

PROJECT SUMMARY

PROJECT NAME:
150-kWe Power Generation in Dual Fuel Mode

CAPITAL COST:
$45,000

DEVELOPER:
Ankur Scientific Energy Technology Pvt., Ltd., India

PROJECT HOST:
M S Rice Industries

GEOGRAPHICAL LOCATION:
Uttar Pradesh, India

TYPE OF ENERGY PROJECT:
Rice husk-based power generation in dual fuel mode

PROJECT COMPLETION YEAR:
2019

The feasibility of biomass is also dependent on technology. Biomass combustion is more feasible for larger capacities while biomass gasification is ideal for small- to medium–sized plants. Given these considerations, the rice mill decided to use a rice husk-fed gasifier system to reduce their dependence on expensive diesel fuel. The gasifier was the best option as it can reduce the diesel consumption by 65%–70%. The power generation cost using gasifier was even lower than the electricity price from the grid. More importantly the feedstock, i.e., rice husk, that was being used in the gasifier was generated from the milling process. Rice husk disposal was no longer a problem and the resource could be used more effectively.

TECHNOLOGY

The 150-kilowatt electrical (kWe) downdraft gasifier with complete gas cleaning and cooling system was found to be suitable to replace the diesel generator. Gasification is the conversion of solid hydrocarboneous fuels (wood/wood waste, bamboo, and various agricultural residues, etc.) into a combustible gas mixture called producer gas or syngas. The gasifier is essentially a chemical reactor where various physical and chemical processes take place and break the solid fuel down into producer gas. The process of generating an ultra clean gas with tar and particulate levels of just a few milligrams per cubic meter of gas begins in the gasifier itself along with the gas cooling and cleaning systems (Figure 40).

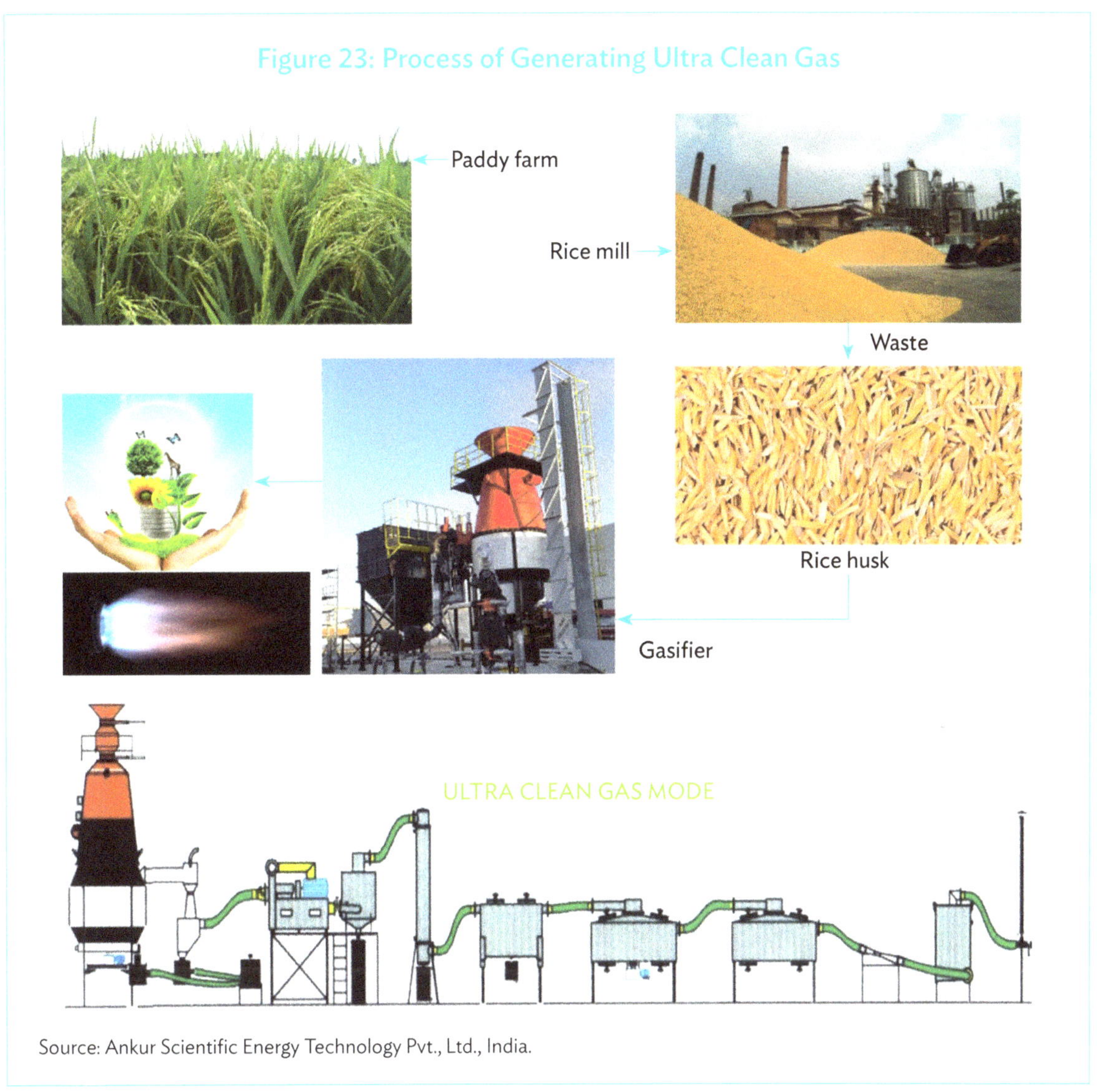

BUSINESS MODEL

The power generation cost was much lower with the installation of gasifier and the savings generated increased the revenue streams of the rice mill. The regular diesel consumption of the rice mill was about 50 liters per hour, which was reduced to approximately 15 liters per hour after the installation of the gasifier system, thereby saving around 35 liters diesel per hour. The following are some relevant figures in the operation of the gasifier system:

(i)   Net power generated in a year - approximately 840 MWh;

(ii)   Rice husk consumption per hour – approximately 210 kilograms;

(iii) Rice husk consumption per annum - approximately 1,260 tons;

(iv)   Diesel consumption with gasifier per annum - approximately 90,000 liters; and

(v)   Unit cost of power generation using gasifier system in dual fuel mode - approximately $0.11 per kWh against cost of power when using 100% diesel mode of about $0.33 per kWh.

FINANCING STRUCTURE

The total project cost was approximately $45,000 with a subsidy coming from the central government of India amounting to approximately $6,500. The financing was done by the rice mill from their internal accrual and they could recover the investment in less than 6 months.

RESULTS

The grid power was unreliable. Thus, the rice mill used a diesel generator to augment its electricity supply. By coupling the rice husk gasifier system to their existing diesel genset in dual fuel mode, the mill could save diesel consumption translating to additional income. The rice mill generated cheaper and cleaner source of power. Rice husk disposal including handling, transportation, etc. is no longer a problem. Regular procurement and storage of large quantity of diesel are no longer necessary.

LESSONS

The gasifier-based power generation system was an excellent investment option for the private rice mill as rice husk is readily available for free. The use of gasifier generated substantial savings to the project host and also seen to have positive and favorable environmental impact.

The use of biomass gasification system via dual fuel mode was a right technology choice as it can displace diesel by 65%–70% or 100% producer gas when the gasifier system was coupled to producer gas or syngas engine generator.

THE DEVELOPER

Ankur Scientific is one of the global leaders in gasification and has vast experience in generating power on dual fuel mode or 100% gas, or host of thermal and/or process heat application. Ankur biomass gasifiers are well known for their extremely clean and consistent gas quality.

KEYWORDS

rice husk gasifier, biomass, gasification, gasifier, producer gas, syn gas, Ankur Scientific, thermal, power, dual fuel, diesel, diesel replacement, diesel saving

FURTHER READING

Ankur. https://www.ankurscientific.com/.

1.11 Australian Bio Fert Small-Scale Biological Fertilizer Demonstration and Product

CONTEXT

Food security is increasingly important as the global population grows and emerging environmental challenges including climate change place pressure on the ecosystem. Many countries are experiencing reductions in per capita arable land for agriculture further creating pressure to increase productivity.

Experience in western countries has shown reduced effectiveness of chemical and synthetic fertilizer and flattening yields as soil is degraded and carbon levels in soil are depleted. The practice of increasing the amounts of chemical fertilizer is no longer achieving increased crop production.

There is growing awareness in soil science, educated farming, and academe that chemical fertilizer is having a long-term damaging impact on soil health and farm production. High and volatile chemical fertilizer prices further impact on the economic viability of food production especially in developing countries.

As the long-term use of chemical fertilizer has impacted negatively on soil health, plants have become more susceptible to disease. This has increased the use of harmful "crop protection" chemicals like glyphosates, which studies have shown to have health issue implications for food production.

PROJECT SUMMARY
PROJECT NAME:
Australian Bio Fert Small-Scale Biological Fertilizer Demonstration and Product Development Facility
CAPITAL COST:
$3.5 million
DEVELOPER:
ideas*/Torreco
PROJECT HOST:
Australian Bio Fert Pty Ltd
GEOGRAPHICAL LOCATION:
Maddingley, Victoria, Australia
TYPE OF ENERGY PROJECT:
Nutrient recovery and recycling Torreco torrefaction and granulation technologies
PROJECT COMPLETION YEAR:
2019

In many developing countries, farmers use compost or animal waste as their main form of nutrient supply. As the humus profile in the soil builds, such practices become sustainable. However, they have inherent logistical and labor efficiency costs. Further, there is a risk of uncontrolled leaching of nutrients into the environment and waterways if not managed properly.

There is a need for sustainable ways to remediate soil and deliver nutrients in plant-available form. Carbon-based slow release fertilizer and soil amendments can help solve these problems by improving both agricultural productivity and building the arable land base in areas where Beach Ridges Interspersed with Swales and other challenging soil conditions predominate.

SOLUTION

Australian Bio Fert has developed a range of organics and carbon-based slow release hybrid fertilizer and soil remediation products. These products deliver nutrients in plant-available form and help sequester carbon in soil, improve soil health, and create an environment where less chemical fertilizer is required. Figure 41 presents a simple diagram of nutrient recovery and recycling process as well as the production of organics-based fertilizer.

Many soil amendment and fertilizer products can be created from a range of base materials. For example, empty fruit bunch is an abundant and problematic waste material that can be converted into a valuable soil amendment and fertilizer, if processed with other nutrient bearing materials.

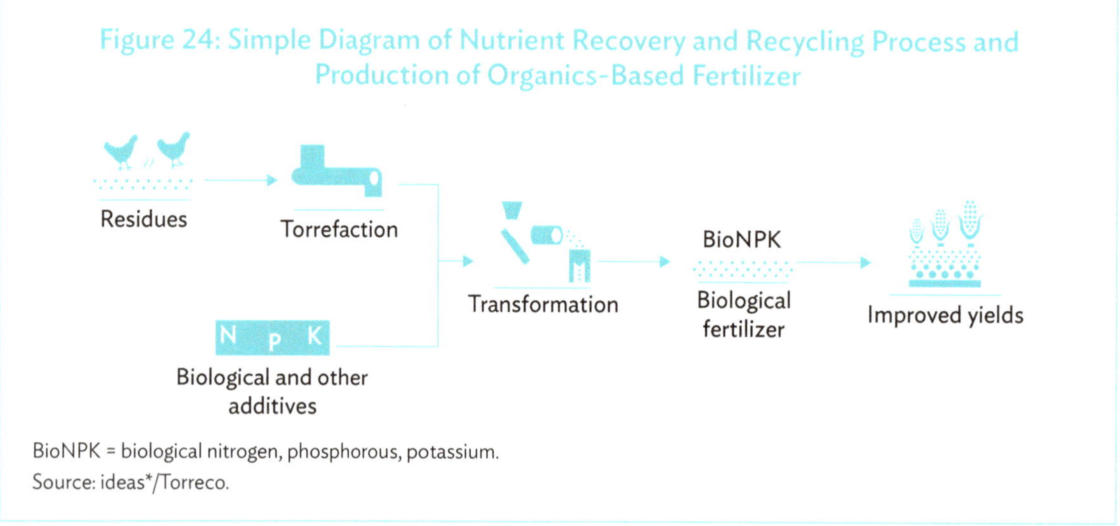

Figure 24: Simple Diagram of Nutrient Recovery and Recycling Process and Production of Organics-Based Fertilizer

BioNPK = biological nitrogen, phosphorous, potassium.
Source: ideas*/Torreco.

TECHNOLOGY

Torrefaction is a thermal process similar in principle to pyrolysis (heating material to elevated temperatures in the absence of oxygen). Torreco and its engineering partner Innovation Development Engineering Administration Services (ideas*)[5] have developed an energy-efficient proprietary technology that is low-cost in terms of both capital and operating expenditures (CAPEX and OPEX) compared to other thermal degradation solutions. The technology enables conversion of low-value inputs to high-value outputs in an energy-efficient process. Figure 42 shows a manufacturing process diagram.

Torrefaction:

(i)   de-waters and densifies (dries material and improves logistics and handling);

(ii)   kills pathogens and stabilizes biologically active materials (important for biosecurity when applying processed bio-waste to land applications); and

(iii)   alters the state of materials (liberates syngas for energy recovery and makes residual material friable "brittle" so it can be easily separated, milled into powders, blended and reformed into marketable value-added products e.g., fertilizer).

---

[5]   ideas*. Melbourne. www.ideaservices.com.au.

Key Advantages

(i)   low CAPEX and OPEX,

(ii)   energy efficiency (syngas generated by the process can power the system reducing reliance on external sources),

(iii)   continuous rather than batch operation (improved efficiency and enables inline processing with other technology solutions),

(iv)   ability to process a range of materials, and

(v)   scalability.

The technology has been developed over 8 years and has been proven at both prototype (50 kilograms per hour) and demonstration (1 tph) scale throughput capacity; a number of materials for a range of applications have been successfully processed.

Combined with other proven technologies such as pyrolysis and granulation, torrefaction forms a number of technology platforms that give access to opportunities to extract inherent value from low-value and often problematic waste materials. A computer image of small-scale biological fertilizer demonstration and product demonstration facility is shown in Figure 43.

In the Australian Bio Fert project, a 750-kilogram (kg) per hour torrefaction system (Figure 44) operates as the front-end organics processing stage, which enables separation of the liquid and solid fractions of the input material. This stage stabilizes the material and deals with biosecurity and pathogen risks. The liquid fraction is blended with other materials to form high-analysis liquid fertilizer and the solid fraction is milled, blended with other materials, and then granulated to form organics and carbon-based slow release fertilizer.

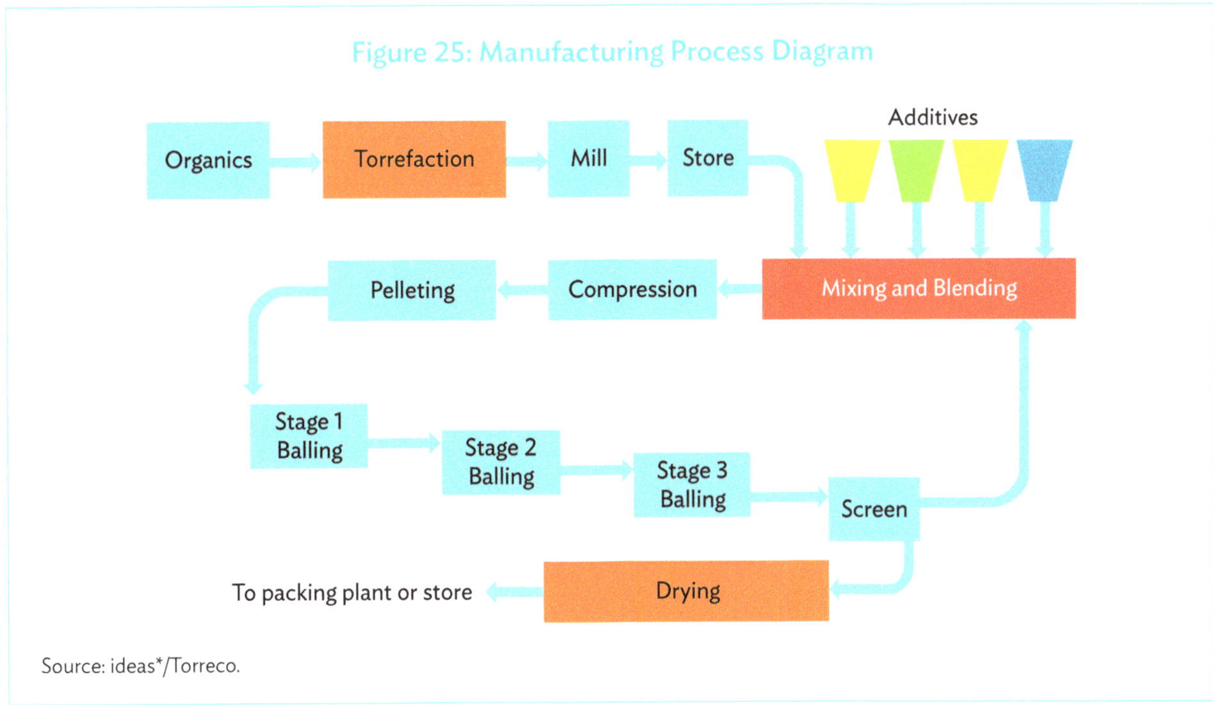

Source: ideas*/Torreco.

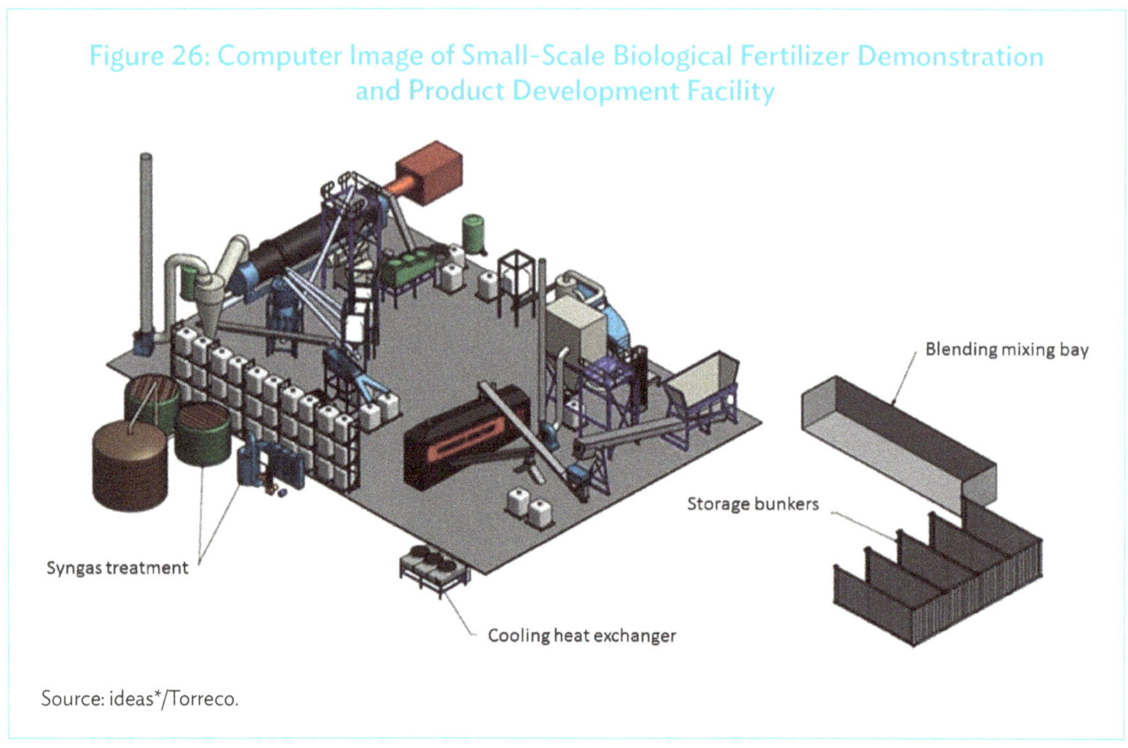

Figure 26: Computer Image of Small-Scale Biological Fertilizer Demonstration and Product Development Facility

Source: ideas*/Torreco.

750 Kilogram/Hour Torreco Torrefier. In the Australian Bio Fert project, a 750-kilogram per hour torrefaction system operates as the front-end organics processing stage, which enables separation of the liquid and solid fractions of the input material (photo by ideas*/Torreco).

Australian Bio Fert Demonstration Plant. The plant utilizes a torrefaction technology that enables conversion of low-value inputs to high-value outputs in an energy-efficient process (photo by ideas*/Torreco).

Organic waste materials such as chicken manure, chicken litter, and dead birds (mortalities) are pre-processed, mixed, homogenized, and sized for delivery to the torrefier. The material enters the torrefaction reaction chamber where it is subjected to temperatures approximately 350°C in a no/low oxygen environment. During the drying process, wet gases are created and passed through a condenser where the nutrient containing liquid is captured. The dry friable solid fraction is further processed by milling, blending with other nutrient bearing materials, and formation into granules for ease of storage and handling.

The computer-controlled production process is efficient with very little waste. The plant requires heat and electricity. The demonstration system is powered by electricity and LPG. Plants can be designed to make use of any available waste heat or solar thermal solutions. Estimated energy requirements for a 64,000-ton fertilizer plant (45,000 ton granules and 19,000 ton liquids) are shown in Table 17 below:

Table 17: Estimated Energy Requirements for a 64,000-Ton Fertilizer Plant

Energy Requirement	Source	Consumption
Torrefier	LPG	53 liters/ton wet organics input
Dryer	LPG	39 liters/ton granules output
Power	Electricity	1,100 kWh for a 64,000-ton plant

kWh = kilowatt-hour, LPG = liquefied petroleum gas.
Source: ideas*/Torreco.

The production plant is designed to operate year-round 24 hours a day. The expected lifetime of the plant is at least 25 years.

BUSINESS MODEL

Australian Bio Fert aims to build company-owned fertilizer plants throughout Australia and pursue joint venture and/or licensing arrangements with third parties in other countries and regions.

The business model is based on providing a mixture of waste management solutions (in some cases on a gate fee model) and the production and sale of value-added products e.g., fertilizer and soil remediation products. There is scope for monetization of carbon sequestration depending on individual countries' laws and regulations.

FINANCING STRUCTURE

Funding for the construction of the demonstration facility and commercialization of the technology has been provided by Australian Bio Fert shareholders, supported by Australian Federal Government Research and Development Tax Incentives, a federal government grant under the Accelerating Commercialisation Programme and a Victorian State Government grant under the Food Source Victoria Programme. The Australian Bio Fert demonstration plant is shown in Figure 45.

RESULTS

Australian Bio Fert has proved the capability and efficacy of the production process. Organics-based agricultural residues such as poultry manure, poultry litter, dead birds (mortalities) have been transformed into value-added products that deliver nutrients to crops in plant-available form. An ongoing program of product trials involving laboratory pot trials and limited field trials in broadacre cropping, pasture, and horticulture have shown the products are effective alternatives to chemical and synthetic fertilizer. For example, a 2017 pasture trial compared Australian Bio Fert liquid and granular products with commercially available alternatives and showed outperformance (Table 18). A number of trials have indicated at least equivalent performance.

Table 18: Extract from 2017 Merrijig Pasture Trials

Pasture Trial	Unit	Control (no fertilizer)	ABF Granule	Superphosphate	ABF-SOL	Seasol
Plot yield	(kg)	4.3	21.8	11.0	15.1	12
Equiv. Yield	t/ha	2.9	14.5	7.3	10.0	8

ABF = Australian Bio Fert, ha = hectare, kg = kilogram, t = ton.
Source: ideas*/Torreco.

Previous trials undertaken by Torreco have shown ability to process other materials such as EFB, municipal green waste, MSW, and abattoir waste.

LESSONS

Nutrient-rich organic waste materials can be converted into high-value fertilizer and soil amendment products. These products can be created and utilized in developing countries to help improve agricultural productivity and remediate degraded land.

THE DEVELOPER

Innovation Development Engineering Administration Services (ideas*) (www.ideaservices.com.au) is an Australian based front-end engineering design business that specializes in materials handling and thermal processes involving treatment of biomass materials. Ideas* has experience bringing new technologies to brownfields manufacturing environments.

Torreco has been formed to house the intellectual property and commercialize an innovative Australian torrefaction technology with applications in waste management, and the conversion of biomass and organic waste materials into value-added energy and fertilizer products. Australian Bio Fert holds a worldwide license to the Torreco torrefaction and granulation technologies as applied to conversion of manure to fertilizer.

KEYWORDS

torrefaction, granulation, Torreco, Australian Bio Fert, biological fertilizer, ideas*[6]

FURTHER READING

Australian Biofert. *Improve Soil Health and Crop Yields.*

Australian Biofert. http://austbiofert.com.au/.

---

[6]   ideas*. Melbourne. www.ideaservices.com.au.

1.12   CBE—Clean Energy Community

CONTEXT

Thailand is considered a leader in renewable energy development in Southeast Asia due to its strong renewable energy sector policy, promotion, and climate change campaign for more than a decade.

In 2015, the Alternative Energy Development Plan 2015–2036[7] announced by Thailand Ministry of Energy set the overall target of increasing the share of renewable energy to 30% in the final energy consumption by 2036. The plan includes the utilization of renewable energy for electricity generation in all forms and technologies. The private sector in Thailand is an important driver to support the sustainable and long-term development of clean energy in the country.

The farming sector is a major contributor to Thailand's economy. Most rice mills are already using rice husks to produce energy. Other agricultural residues, however, have often just been wasted. The Clean Energy Community (CBE) project has been designed to be able

<table>
<tr><td colspan="1">PROJECT SUMMARY</td></tr>
<tr><td>PROJECT NAME:
CBE—Clean Energy Community</td></tr>
<tr><td>CAPITAL COST:
$11 million</td></tr>
<tr><td>DEVELOPER:
SBANG Sustainable Energies</td></tr>
<tr><td>PROJECT HOST:
SBANG Sustainable Energies</td></tr>
<tr><td>GEOGRAPHICAL LOCATION:
Phrompiram, Phitsanulok, Thailand</td></tr>
<tr><td>TYPE OF ENERGY PROJECT:
Biomass to energy waste from agriculture</td></tr>
<tr><td>PROJECT COMPLETION YEAR:
2018</td></tr>
</table>

SBANG CBE Plant. The plant utilizes different types of biomass to ensure the steady supply of fuel (photo by SBANG Sustainable Energies).

---

7   Government of Thailand, Ministry of Energy. 2015. Alternative Energy Development Plan: AEDP2015. Department of Renewable Energy Development and Energy Efficiency. September.

to use other agricultural wastes to generate additional income to local farmers. The project was named Clean Energy Community as it benefits a local community while generating electricity. Figure 46 shows SBANG CBE plant.

SOLUTION

Some projects in the region have stalled in recent years due to non-availability or increase in the cost of biomass, which is only specific to certain technologies. The CBE plant makes use of technology that can handle and incinerate different types of feedstock at varying sizes and moisture content, including those with difficult fuel characteristics such as corrosiveness and high ash content. This approach assures fuel supply reliability. The technology solution for this project was based on locally available feedstock and operational experience of SBANG Sustainable Energies. The project was also designed with smaller system capacity (4.9 MWe) to have smaller requirement for biomass.

Operating a biomass power plant, especially for steam thermal technology requires sufficient amount of raw water. The raw water is used for processed steam and for cooling tower. A 10-MW power plant normally requires around 100 m³ of water per day to produce 1 MW of electricity. This plant would therefore require approximately 500 m³ of water per day.

The project's land area includes space for two water reservoirs with a combined capacity of 120,000 m³. This amount of water is sufficient to provide continuous supply of raw water for 8 months' operation, even without rain. The rainy season in Thailand usually lasts for 6 months on the average and the reservoirs can be filled by rainwater and from run-off water from nearby hills. In addition, plant is located near a river basin of Phitsanulok province, thus water supply is continuously available.

The involvement of local communities is also one of the success factors of the project. Local farmers can have additional income and the residents are assured that the plant will not pollute their environment. The community participated in the early stage of the project and farmers in the area even offered to supply biomass feedstock such as wood chip, sawdust, corncob, and sugarcane leaves. As the biomass system can make use of different types of feedstock, farmers can diversify their crops, hence the opportunity to have more income.

The water for the cooling tower is sourced from reservoirs located in the project site. The water recovered from the power plant is also being treated on-site for reuse, achieving a zero discharge of wastewater.

CBE Power Plant—Compact Design. The CBE plant makes use of technology that can handle and incinerate different types of feedstock at varying sizes and moisture content (photo by SBANG Sustainable Energies).

TECHNOLOGY

Biomass fuel from agricultural waste is delivered by trucks to the plant from a range of small-scale suppliers in the area. A front loader is used to transport feedstock to a mixing area, which will go to a moving floor system, feeding a chain conveyor to an elevated dosing bunker located at front of the boiler. Two double screws are used for even dosing of the fuel mix into feed chutes of spreader feeders into the combustion chamber. The fuel enters the combustion area and partially ignited while in suspension.

The combustion system is based on a water-cooled vibrating grate, a proven low-cost solution for multiple types of biomass fuels. The water cooling of the grate ensures that no ashes will soften and stick to the grate surface. The vibration of the grate in different time intervals determines the speed of the fuel bed traveling through different air zones, ensuring a complete combustion before bottom ash drops into a wet chain conveyor. The grate is modularized so it can be removed from the boiler quickly.

Preheated primary air is used as main source of oxygen for the combustion. If the fuel moisture is too high, a flue gas recirculation system will be used to increase the amount of hot gases without increasing the oxygen content. Secondary air nozzles above the combustion chamber create turbulence in the combustion zone to ensure complete combustion. This combustion system relies largely on the combustion of fuels while in suspension, similar to a fluidized bed boiler. This reduces the required grate and boiler size compared to other grate type boilers. The technology design and the CBE combustion process are shown in Figures 47 and 48, respectively.

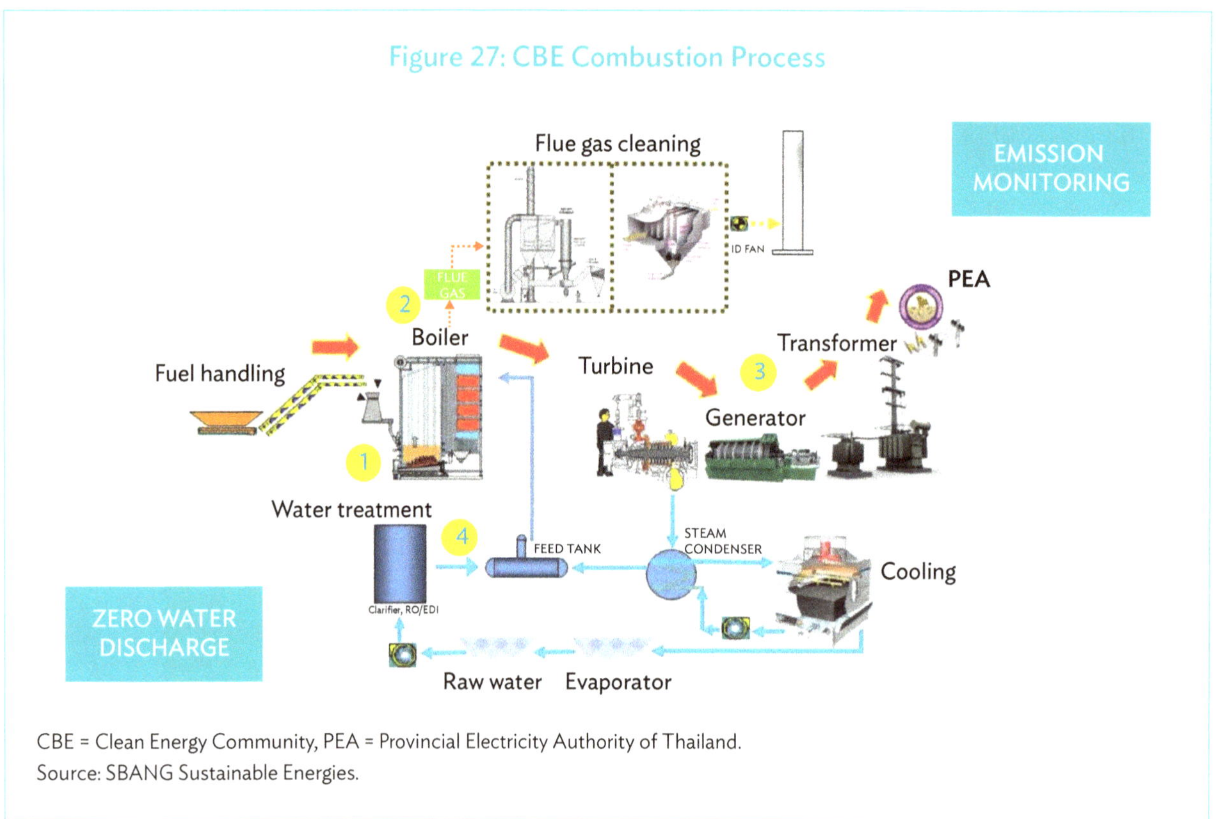

Figure 27: CBE Combustion Process

CBE = Clean Energy Community, PEA = Provincial Electricity Authority of Thailand.
Source: SBANG Sustainable Energies.

The hot flue gas is going through the boiler convection, superheater, and economizer sections. The flue gas is then cleaned in an electrostatic filter system, catching the fly ash, which can be used as fertilizer or other purposes.

The boiler system is used to transfer thermal energy from hot flue gases to heat up water and produce high-pressure steam that will drive the turbine generator. The power produced by the generator is fed to the plant's medium voltage transformer station and then to the power grid.

BUSINESS MODEL

The schematic diagram of CBE business model is illustrated in Figure 49 below.

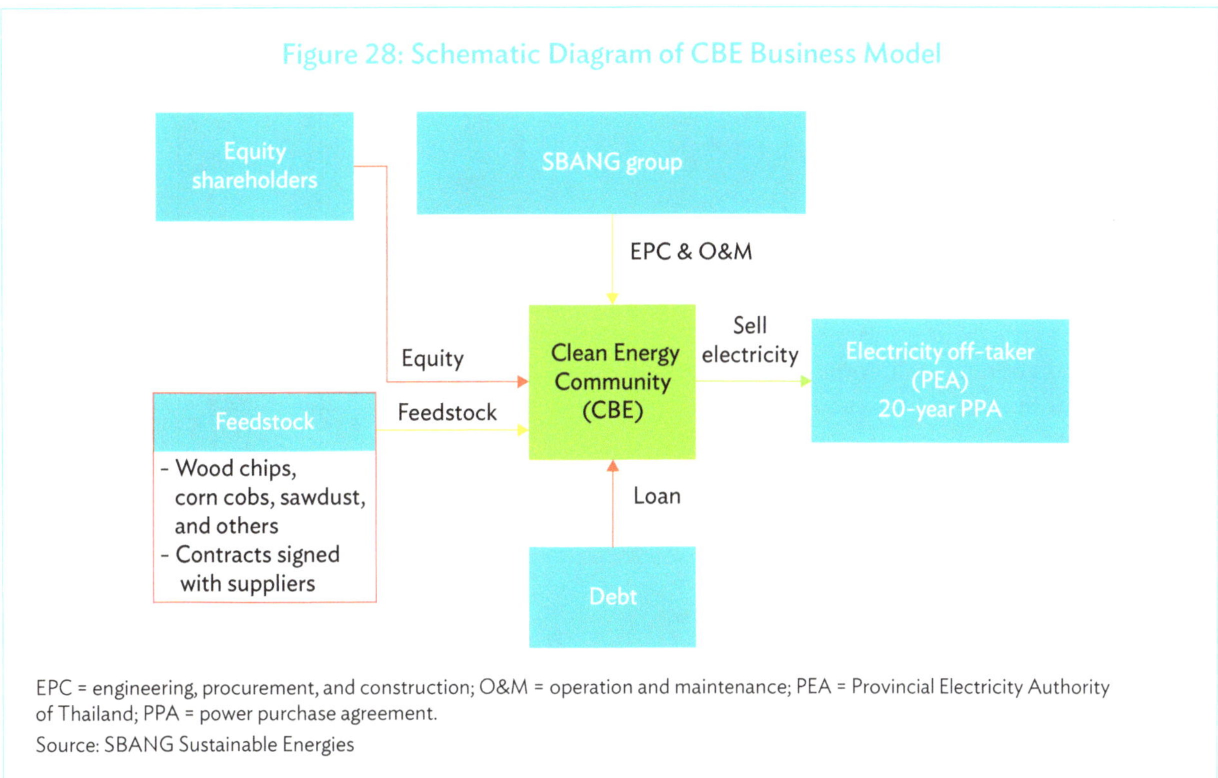

Figure 28: Schematic Diagram of CBE Business Model

EPC = engineering, procurement, and construction; O&M = operation and maintenance; PEA = Provincial Electricity Authority of Thailand; PPA = power purchase agreement.
Source: SBANG Sustainable Energies

FINANCING STRUCTURE

The only revenue stream assumed in the business model is from a 20-year power purchase agreement (PPA) signed by the SBANG Sustainable Energies with the Provincial Electricity Authority (PEA) (Figure 50). The PPA stipulates a cost of electricity at B4.54/kWh or $0.138 /kWh.[8] The net present value and internal rate of return over the project lifetime are $6.95 million and 19%, respectively. The project aims for the continuous operation of the plant and attain high efficiency to minimize operations and maintenance costs. A sensitivity analysis was made to determine the impact of fuel price fluctuation and plant efficiency and determine at which point the project is still viable.

---

[8]   As of August 2018.

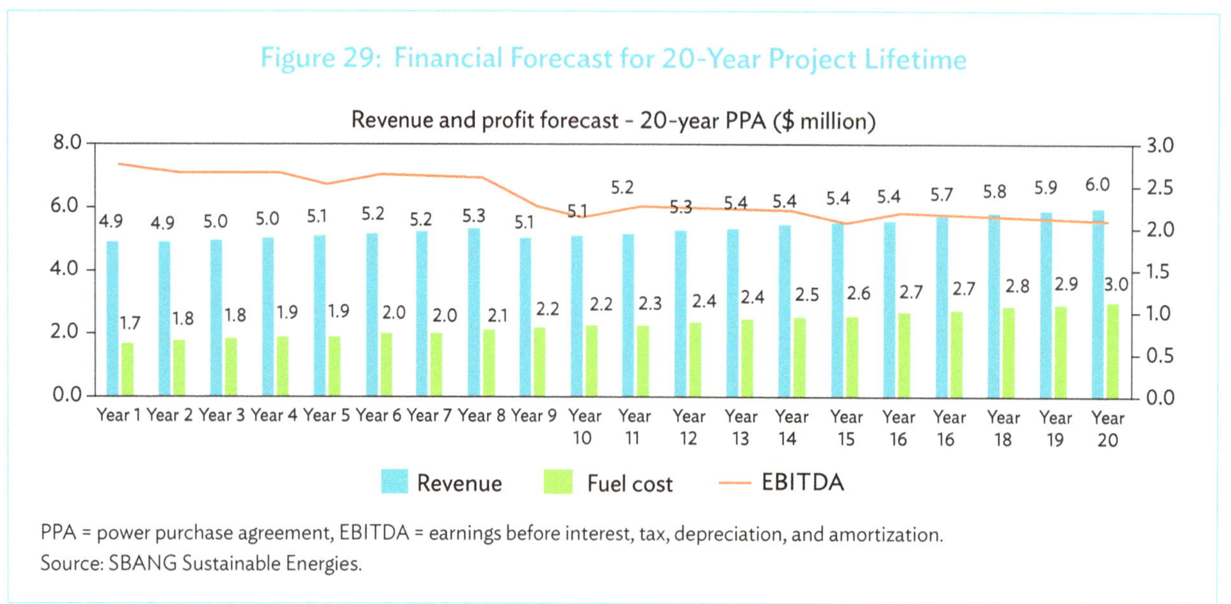

Figure 29: Financial Forecast for 20-Year Project Lifetime

Revenue and profit forecast - 20-year PPA ($ million)

PPA = power purchase agreement, EBITDA = earnings before interest, tax, depreciation, and amortization.
Source: SBANG Sustainable Energies.

RESULTS

The CBE project has been developed with the involvement of the local community in mind. Farmers in the area earn additional income from the project as they are the source of biomass fuel (A stack of rice hull to be used for the project is shown in Figure 51). The project created a long-term employment opportunities and sustainable income for skilled workforce in the area.

The investors also gain a reasonable amount of profit and financiers are exposed to low-level of risks. Reliable technology solutions ensure continuous plant operation and efficient performance of the power plant.

The small size of the project and the use of different types of biomass ensure the steady supply of fuel. The project also has other benefits such as the use of locally available biomass, zero discharge of wastewater, and low levels of emissions. At the macro level, the use of locally available agricultural wastes to produce energy also reduces Thailand's dependence on fossil fuels and stabilizes the weak power grid in the province.

Rice Hull Waste. Farmers in the area earn additional income from the project as they are the source of biomass fuel (photo by SBANG Sustainable Energies).

On 19 September 2019, CBE has been validated by Thailand Greenhouse Gas Management Organization or TGO (Public Organization) and registered in the Thailand Voluntary Emission Reduction Program, recognizing CBE's contribution in reducing the world's GHG emission by using biomass for electricity generation.

LESSONS

Community involvement from the start of the project resulted to the project's smooth implementation. SBANG Sustainable Energies maintains continued dialogue with the community and stresses the important role they play throughout the operation phase.

The project carefully chose the technology to be used taking into consideration factors such as multi-fuel feedstock, fuel handling, and feeding and combustion systems. The technology is a critical to ensure smooth operation of a biomass power plant while maintaining minimal disruption.

Management of water resources is a key factor for stable operation of any power plant and may become a major issue especially during dry seasons. The project design should include water collection and storage during the rainy season. Additional backup from other alternative sources may be considered for continuous operation of the power plant.

THE DEVELOPER

SBANG Sustainable Energies is a Thai engineering company. SBANG serves as project developer, owner, and operator of several WtE solutions in Southeast Asia and Australia. SBANG has built 10 existing biomass power plants, which were established since 2004.

KEYWORDS

agricultural wastes, steam thermal technology, flue gas, zero water discharge, SBANG Sustainable Energies, CBE power plant

FOR FURTHER READING

SBANG Group. https://www.sbang-group.com/

Thailand Greenhouse Gas Management Organization. www.tgo.or.th.

SBANG Group. Waste to Values. https://docs.wixstatic.com/ugd/bf25eb_ b30bb1ff6e464028b830af6645626745.pdf.

1.13   ID Gasifiers Coconut Shell-Fueled Module—Coconut Technology Centre Development

CONTEXT

The Kokonut Pacific Solomon Islands (KPSI) is a production network established by Kokonut Pacific Pty Ltd (KPP), an Australia-based company. KPSI is comprised of approximately 60 village-based virgin coconut oil mills which, together, draw coconuts from over 1,000 small-hold farmers. These mills produce around 200 metric tons (Mt) of oil for export each year. Each mill processes approximately 1,000 coconuts per day and these, in turn, produce around 50 kgs of oil per day. The oil is then consolidated in Honiara. These small mills use simple drying tables to prepare the copra for oil extraction, which is then completed in a hand-operated press. The tables are heated through direct combustion of coconut shell, this practice created an uncomfortable and unhealthy work environment due to the smoke.

KPSI is involved in a coconut replanting program with their farmers and hopes that this will reduce the impact of the coconut rhinoceros beetle that breeds in rotting coconut stems. This work involves the removal of overmature coconut palms and could involve an estimated 2,500 coconut palms per year. This would represent an estimated 600 Mt of coconut stem lump charcoal annually, a potential product identified that could provide an economic return as part of the necessary management. A training and research organization called the Solomon Islands Coconut Technology Centre in Honiara was established to consolidate and support this work. Electricity cost in the Solomon Islands was very high and an impediment to business.

PROJECT SUMMARY
PROJECT NAME:
ID Gasifiers Coconut Shell Fueled Module—Coconut Technology Centre Development Program
CAPITAL COST:
$14,388
DEVELOPER:
ID Gasifiers Pty Ltd
PROJECT HOST:
Kokonut Pacific Pty Ltd
GEOGRAPHICAL LOCATION:
Honiara, Solomon Islands
TYPE OF ENERGY PROJECT:
Biomass to heat and power applications
PROJECT COMPLETION YEAR:
2016

SOLUTION

It was identified that a coconut shell-fueled charcoal-producing gasifier could provide a multifaceted solution providing clean heat and power and charcoal production.

ID Gasifiers Pty Ltd (IDG), a business located in the same region as KPP's Australian base of operations in Queanbeyan, New South Wales, was selected as the technology provider. IDG had demonstrated a gasifier on the lawns of Parliament House Canberra only a few years earlier and was actively developing it for commercial application. Meetings and technology demonstrations were arranged and the use of coconut shell as feedstock was used for testing.

IDG Gasifier at the Site. A coconut shell-fueled charcoal-producing gasifier could provide a multifaceted solution providing clean heat and power and charcoal production (photo by ID Gasifiers Pty Ltd.).

KPP had successfully developed the concept of lesser labor-intensive equipment for its operations, well suited to the Pacific region where power was expensive or simply not available. KPP wanted to manually operate a small plant as labor was readily available—creating employment that no matter how menial, was seen as beneficial. IDG developed its gasifier from its own unique perspectives and had a different view and experience to its peers in the industry, starting with its first system at 200 kg/hour (not bench scale). The system could be scaled down, but IDG's concern was this would introduce additional fuel pre-processing requirements of fine sizing, that is the coconut shell would need to be crushed and not used as is. IDG also developed a simple mechanical feeder allowing several hours of fuel to be held requiring only minimal supervision and labor. A compromise design of only 15 kWe was made by IDG to meet KPP's stated requirement. The system is capable of using an inclined ramp carrying a hopper that can be moved using a hand winch requiring loading every 15 minutes. The installed gasifier is shown in Figure 52.

TECHNOLOGY

Gasification is a thermal process that turns woody and/or organic materials into energy-rich gas by heating the solid fuel under controlled conditions. As a long-established technology, a popular misconception then is the technology was mature. To a degree this was true for large coal-fed systems that came in configurations such as fluidized bed that worked at scale when coupled with boilers. For small scale, it was instead a last resort and was difficult to manage and maintain even on charcoal as fuel. Robust functional designs for biomass gasifiers were much sought but seldom achieved.

IDG Gasifier. A gasifier was set up for demonstration and promotion of the technology through the Solomon Islands Coconut Technology Centre (ID Gasifiers Pty Ltd.).

Typical problems included:

(i)   Gas production was not uniform in quality, quantity, or energy value. Most systems required lock hoppers for sealing during operation. This resulted in internal conditions changing over time as particle size reduced and gas flow pathways became restricted, moisture was driven off, and temperature gas composition values altered.

(ii)   A big problem was dead zones within the gasifier bed where variable porosity leads to non-uniform gas flows and heat distribution through the fuel, creating changing and often sub-optimal gasifying conditions as well as creation of undesirable tars—usually long-chain hydrocarbons that can clog pipes and foul engines.

(iii) The ash fusion temperature (where inorganic components of the feed stock melt and clump together forming clinker and slag) of most biomass is below that required for thermal disassociation of complex organic molecules, negating one of the greatest advantages and rendering systems maintenance intensive resulting in variable performance.

IDG had solved these and other operational problems with unique design. The closest description in the literature would be a modified stratified downdraft gasifier. The IDG system can handle higher moisture contents than usual and continually automatically remove char largely before it was reduced to mineral ash. IDG gasifiers can also handle clinkers as they formed, allowing much wider range of feed stock particle size (field friendly). The photo of IDG gasifier is shown in Figure 53 while its schematic process is illustrated in Figure 54. The fuel column is open to atmosphere during operation making

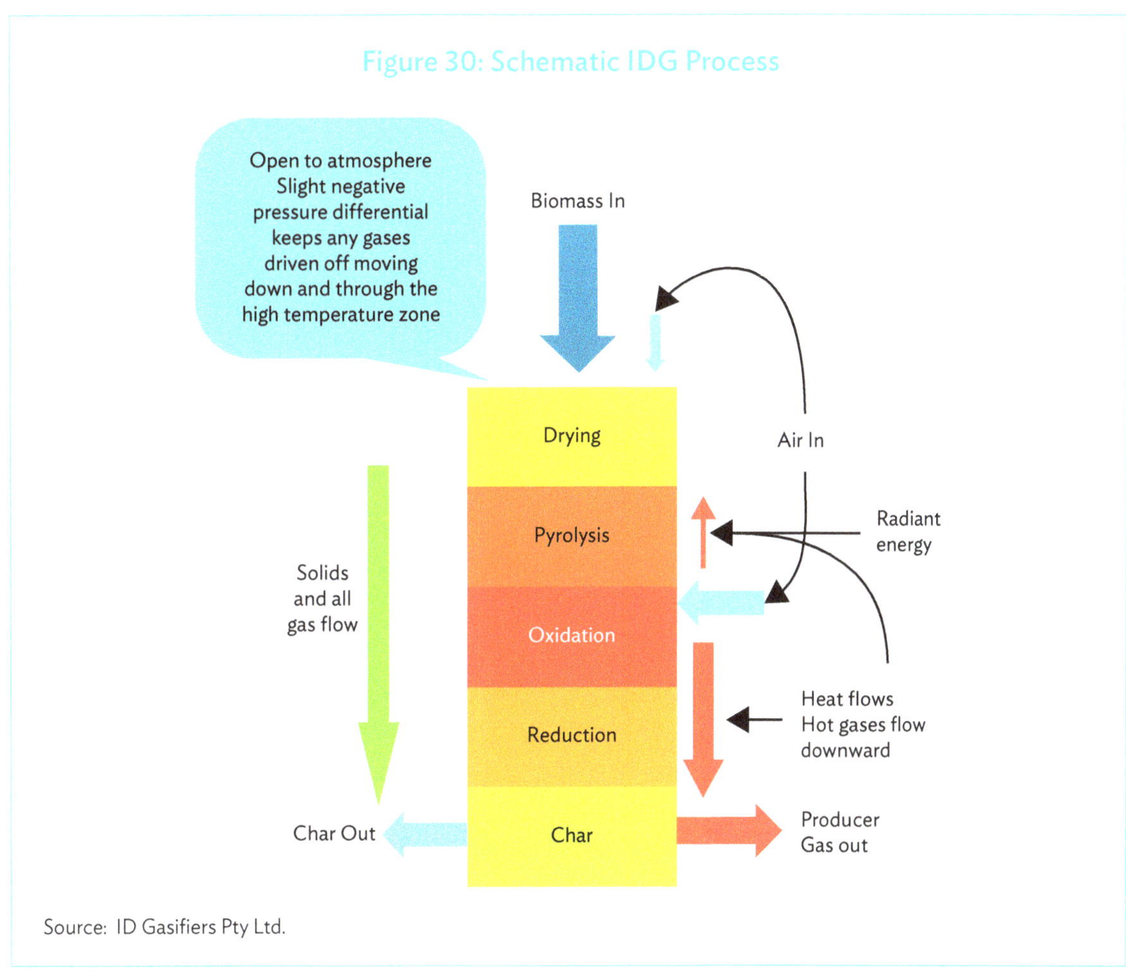

Source: ID Gasifiers Pty Ltd.

feeding easy and continuous with standard low-cost conveyors. As fuel descends down the column under gravity, it passes through several temperature zones where all organic materials are ultimately reduced to their simplest chemical forms: producer gas, carbon monoxide (a fuel gas), hydrogen (a fuel gas), and < 1% methane and trace hydrocarbons (fuel gases) mixed with inert CO_2 (created during the process), N_2 and argon (from the air used as the source of oxygen) and low volatile matter charcoal with high porosity and fixed carbon content.

BUSINESS MODEL

The basic business model envisaged was for a system creating cascading values:

(i)   Management of coconut shell waste in a way that provided a clean working environment and improved productivity and safety.

(ii)   Production of easily managed clean heat for operating the drying tables, improving uniformity of product.

   (iii) Production of electricity for the site to allow lower cost operation of modern offices, workplace, and use of packing equipment.

   (iv) Production of new product in the form of char for a range of existing and emerging markets.

   (v) Provision of end use for waste trees that needed to be removed to better manage pests and ensure a future coconut supply.

The purpose of the pilot trial was to quantify these values. It was expected that a suitable diesel genset would be purchased for the project in the first instance, one with a known capacity to be modified for dual fuel operation using producer gas. Ultimately, it was expected that an industrial spark ignition genset would replace this allowing 100% operation on producer gas.

The project and system were structured to allow change as performance on-site was evaluated and system fine-tuned to suit the circumstances.

FINANCING STRUCTURE

IDG was carrying most of the cost and risk in the first instance. A low commencement cost of around $4,170 (A$3,000)[9] and monthly lease of $695 (A$500) was charged. This was below system cost, but IDG had made the decision to contribute because of the nature of the project and the promise to use the system for demonstration and promotion through the Solomon Islands Coconut Technology Centre. KPP was responsible for labor and other operational costs as well as shipping. The lease had a final (modest) purchase option and if this was not implemented then the unit had to be returned to IDG.

RESULTS

Initial results were disappointing for IDG. Very little of the originally planned project was carried out after the unit arrived on-site as there appeared to be local management resistance. The unit was not unpacked out of the container for 6 months. When it was, it caused immediate interest from neighbors who wanted to connect to any generator it would run, but the system as specified was too small for this and in any case no generator had been purchased as had been discussed and none were initially available. No shedding was provided initially and the unit was run in the open. It was reported to be working fine and successfully heating the drying table although an orange flame was observed instead of a largely transparent one. The system was put down to higher moisture content fuel on-site and plans were made to develop a fuel drying system.

---

9   $1:A$1.39 as of 31 December 2016 (Source: https://forex.adb.org/fx_rate/getRates).

Two breakdowns were reported:

(i) The first was the valve between the gasifier and char bin. This was a 3-inch brass gate valve, which was closed during char bin emptying to prevent air ingress to the gasifier and allow it to continue to operate while the bin was emptied and resealed. Pictures of the valve showed it to have the shaft sheared off but with the valve in the full open position. It turned out the operator had opened the valve after cleaning the char bin as per normal but continued turning the handle after it reached the stop position till the handle broke off. A new valve was supplied by IDG.

Produced Biochar. Rather than the coconut shell being wasted, the project was able to convert it to biochar which is valued at $8.70 per day (photo by ID Gasifiers Pty Ltd.).

(ii) The second was more serious as it was reported the fan and piping had tarred up and the unit stopped completely. A preliminary assessment was made based on observations from the operator on-site. It was surmised the problem was a blocked pipe and components were then made in Australia to replace them. An IDG member traveled to the Coconut Technology Center to install and train additional local staff. The following were the findings of the IDG personnel:

- Apart from the pipe blockage, the systems fan housing was broken at two points and misaligned by one hole so fan could not function. All lower guards were off and in-feed not aligned.
- Training the new operators commenced during this repair and continued then over 2 days using both coconut shell and palm log chunks (sized with chainsaw and small ax).

The system was subsequently tested by an engineer engaged by KPP and its affiliates to prepare a report on the gasifier. All testing was done in the absence of IDG personnel. The outcomes were reported as very positive as reported below:

"The indicative data from the collaborative work with ID Gasifiers suggests that even with an un-optimized system and inexperienced team, the system could provide over 30% in fuel savings, and generate good quality hot air and hot water to assist with virgin coconut oil processing. Compared to the open combustion of shells to provide heating, the system provided clean smoke-free gas for the oil dryers. Compared to electricity from the local power utility at around SI$7/kWh ($0.87), the system provided electricity at less than SI$1/kWh ($0.12). Rather than the coconut shell being wasted, it was converted to biochar (Figure 55), which is valued at SI$70/day ($8.70). The technical and engineering capacity of the ID Gasifiers team is a good example of Australian expertise that can create significant economic development and support a viable biochar Industry in a Pacific context."[10]

---

[10] $1:SBD8.23 as of 31 December 2016 (Source: https://forex.adb.org/fx_rate/getRates).

The results above were after taking into account the labor-intensive nature of the pilot setup. Also the genset testing was conducted with a second-hand air cooled diesel (donated) and was not able to be readily modified to accept producer gas as the air intakes also formed part of the engine cooling. Actual data showed even with a very simple hose connection under which the gas flow could not be changed or matched to engine needs diesel consumption over the same period was reduced from 2.2 liters (diesel only operation) to 1.42 liters (diesel with producer gas), or 65% of its normal consumption (35% reduction).

LESSONS

(i)   **Operator error is a function of training, follow-up, and system design.**

- During IDG visit to the site and discussion with local operators, it was discovered that it had been run previously without the primary air intake open. This had been the primary cause of the pipe blockage flare as the unit had continued to function with only secondary air coming down the fuel column, but sub-optimally, producing larger amounts of liquid condensates as well as tars. It was also the reason for the fan to be disassembled.

- After IDG personnel repaired it and conducted fresh training, the unit performed as originally specified when run only by the newly trained operators and this was commented on as being substantially different to what they had been seeing until then.

- IDG holds the view that such issues are ultimately the developer's responsibility, blaming the operator does not ensure system acceptance and uptake. Training protocols have been revised, system design has taken into account the experience and applied changes to make it very easy to manage appropriately and more difficult to run it any other way.

(ii)   **Jobs resulting from the installation of the gasifier must be meaningful and rewarding.**

- The IDG member developed good rapport with trainees and other locals. He noted that the hand preparation of fuel being carried out was tedious and, in his view, unsafe. This was confirmed by his new connections that found the work unsatisfying and avoided where possible. At the same time, the locals involved were very excited at what the system could do for their communities.

- System should be designed for the coconut shell as delivered rather than specifying additional grinding and preparation.

- A buffer storage or fuel delivery should be included so the system can run unattended for at least 4 hours, but preferably longer, allowing workers to do other value adding tasks resulting from its availability, other than just running the system.

- IDG has since designed what it refers to as the "Islander" model from the pilot experience.

(i)   **Circular economy not circular problems.**

- While the IDG member was there, a problem had become apparent with a genset that had been acquired being used to supplement site power. This was initially blamed on the gasifier by the local manager until it was pointed out that the gasifier was not and never had been connected. It was subsequently found that it had been incorrectly wired as no qualified electrician had been available. There was no understanding of site loads or generator management. Connecting the gasifier to it subsequently reduced noise and seemed to smooth engine response.

- The islands have plenty of good mechanics but few electricians. This can be addressed on the gasifier by having an independent dual fuel producer gas or diesel or producer gas or petrol engine-driven hydraulics for parasitic load and light site loads rather than electrics for system operation, making it fully stand alone. Accompanying generators must be set up as part of complete package with properly wired and labeled outlets for local connection. There must also be an understanding of power management and generator limitations or failures and excessive maintenance costs will be frequent.

THE DEVELOPER

IDG is a privately held company established in 2013 and headquartered at Colinton, New South Wales. The core business of IDG is the manufacture and application development of thermal processing equipment to generate electricity and process heat by a proprietary technology using an array of organic waste and other solid, renewable feed stocks. The proprietary processing technology and manufacturing protocols are wholly managed by IDG. IDG technology has been extensively demonstrated to industry.

IDG has real-world experience and can provide solutions with scale-appropriate plant to match client requirements. They work directly with clients to design custom solutions either to resolve a waste issue (transform to resource) or to meet process heat or energy demands.

KEYWORDS

gasifier, virgin coconut oil, producer gas, ID Gasifier, Kokonut Pacific Pty Ltd.

FURTHER READING

F. Sanders and P. Taylor. 2018. *Beyond Coconuts, Expanding Village-Scale Biochar Production in the Pacific*. Wagga, NSW.

AgriFutures Australia. *The Australia New Zealand Biochar Conference 2018 Conference Proceedings*. https://www.agrifutures.com.au/wp-content/uploads/2018/10/18-039.pdf.

1.14   Sumilao Farm Waste to Energy

CONTEXT

San Miguel Foods Inc. (SMFI) is a subsidiary of San Miguel PureFoods (SMPF), the food subsidiary of San Miguel Corporation. SMPF currently is the largest food company in the Philippines, with a vast network of offices; farms; and manufacturing, processing, and distribution facilities.

SMFI owns and operates a hog farm in Sumilao, Bukidnon (Sumilao Farm) with a capacity of 4,400 sows. The farm itself is engaged in the production of piglets and market hogs, which involves the process of breeding, farrowing, and growing. At the time that the hog farm was being constructed, Sumilao Farm requested a proposal from Solutions Using Renewable Energy (SURE), Inc. for a WtE project that will make use of its farm wastewater to free itself from the responsibility of putting up its own waste water treatment facility. SURE responded to the said request and submitted a project proposal.

<table>
<tr><td colspan="2">PROJECT SUMMARY</td></tr>
<tr><td colspan="2">PROJECT NAME:</td></tr>
<tr><td colspan="2">Sumilao Farm Waste to Energy</td></tr>
<tr><td colspan="2">CAPITAL COST:</td></tr>
<tr><td colspan="2">$4.7 million</td></tr>
<tr><td colspan="2">DEVELOPER:</td></tr>
<tr><td colspan="2">SURE Eco Energy Philippines, Inc. (SURE Eco)</td></tr>
<tr><td colspan="2">PROJECT HOST:</td></tr>
<tr><td colspan="2">San Miguel PureFoods</td></tr>
<tr><td colspan="2">GEOGRAPHICAL LOCATION:</td></tr>
<tr><td colspan="2">Sumilao, Bukidnon, Philippines</td></tr>
<tr><td colspan="2">TYPE OF ENERGY PROJECT:</td></tr>
<tr><td colspan="2">Livestock waste to energy</td></tr>
<tr><td colspan="2">PROJECT COMPLETION YEAR:</td></tr>
<tr><td colspan="2">2016</td></tr>
</table>

SOLUTION

SURE proposed to develop a WtE facility that will treat the wastewater coming from SMFI using anaerobic digestion to produce biogas that will then be used as fuel to generate electricity. San Miguel will provide a 4-hectare land about a kilometer away from the farm and drainage pipes to convey the wastewater to the anaerobic digester plant. The initial plan was that a 600-kW biogas generator will be installed the farms load of about 300 kW on average. As the expected power generation will reach 850 kW, a PPA

Sumilao Biogas Plant. The facility will treat the wastewater coming from San Miguel Foods, Inc. using anaerobic digestion to produce biogas that will be used as fuel to generate electricity (photo by Sure Eco).

with the local distribution utility was negotiated and secured. Instead of receiving power from the anaerobic digester plant, it was proposed that SURE Eco will sell the generated electricity to the grid and SMFI will get a rebate per kWh sold to the distribution utility, which was about the same as the savings it would realize. Figure 56 shows the Sumilao biogas plant in Bukidnon, Philippines.

TECHNOLOGY

The basic design and process of Sumilao Farm Waste-to-Energy project is described in Figure 57:

Pretreatment

The wastewater from the hog farm flows through a 1-km drainage pipe toward the sump pit inside the WtE plant. The wastewater is then pumped to a drum thickener that will remove much of the liquid and increase the solid content of the wastewater that will then go to the digesters. This is to improve the efficiency of the digesters by increasing the solids retention time. Before feeding into the primary digester, the wastewater passes through a heat exchanger and increase the temperature of the substrate in the digester to about 38°C, increasing further the digestion efficiency. The waste heat from the engine cooling system is used as the heat source.

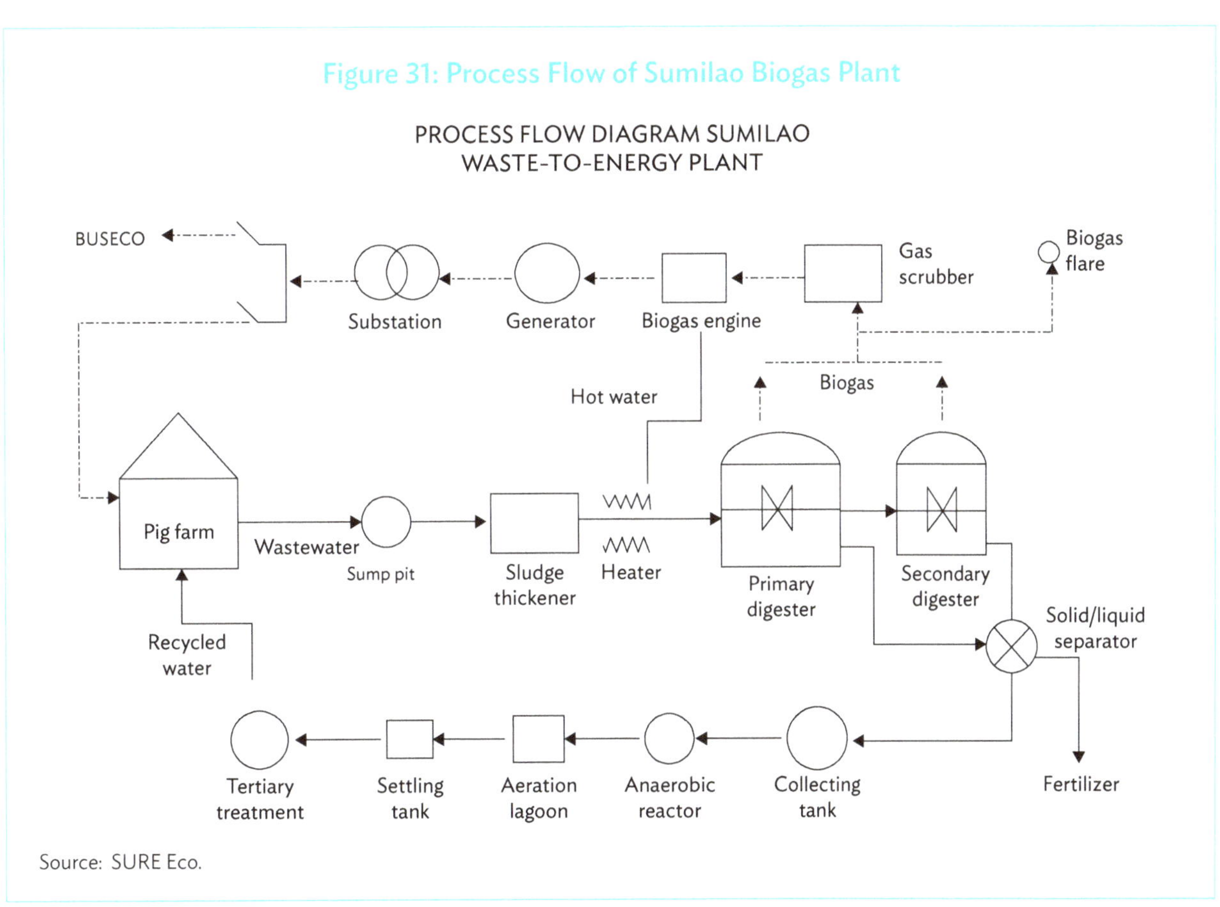

Figure 31: Process Flow of Sumilao Biogas Plant

Source: SURE Eco.

Anaerobic Digestion

The primary (4,400 m³) and secondary (2,800 m³) digesters are stirred at preset intervals. This provides better contact between fresh wastewater feed and methanogenic bacteria inside the digesters. The tanks are also provided with hydraulic recirculation, i.e., the substrate from the bottom part of the tanks are recirculated back through the influent pipeline using a pump, this is also a way of stirring.

As the primary digester is being fed with fresh wastewater, it overflows to the secondary digester where further digestion occurs. On the other hand, the secondary digester also overflows and goes to the collection tank. Biogas is generated in both primary and secondary digesters and is captured and stored in the double membrane covers of the tanks.

Biogas Utilization

Before the biogas produced is fed to the gas engines, it passes through a chemical gas scrubber that uses caustic soda to react with and remove the very corrosive hydrogen sulfide (H_2S) present in the biogas. Part of the gas scrubbing is the removal of the moisture from the biogas by means of a chiller.

The cleaned biogas is then fed to the gas engine using a gas blower to attain the required pressure. An electric generator (925 kW) is coupled to the gas engine to produce electricity at 440 volts. The power substation stepped ups the voltage to 13.8 kilovolts so it can be fed to the primary line of the local distribution utility.

A gas flare is provided such that when power generation is not operational, the excess biogas is combusted. This is better than releasing biogas to the atmosphere as biogas contains about 60% methane that is 20 times more harmful as GHG compared to CO_2 which is a by-product of combustion.

Sludge Treatment

The recirculation system is also installed to remove some of the solids that accumulate at the bottom of the digesters using the same pump. The removed sludge passes through a solid-liquid separator machine. The solids collected is sold directly to farmers or used as raw material for fertilizer production done inside the plant. The liquid then goes to the collection tank for further treatment.

Secondary Wastewater Treatment

The water from the collection tank is pumped to the bottom of the anaerobic reactor that contains polyvinyl chloride (PVC) fillers where anaerobic bacteria populate. The filler material provides greater contact surface such that as the water goes upward, the bacteria can digest much of the remaining undigested solids in the water. A small amount of biogas is also produced and captured at the top of the reactor and then goes to the biogas pipeline.

The reactor overflow goes to an open lagoon for aerobic treatment then goes to another lagoon where remaining solids in the water settle. At this point, the quality of water will pass the standards for discharging into the river.

Under consideration is the recycling of water back to the hog farm. In that case, additional treatment system will be installed before the treated water is pumped back to the farm for reuse.

BUSINESS MODEL

The project is under an 8-year build-operate-transfer agreement between SMFI and SURE Eco. SMFI did not spend anything but provided the 4-hectare site for the WtE plant at minimal rental fee. SURE Eco is responsible for financing the project, as well as its construction and operation. The electricity generated by the plant will be sold to the local distribution utility under a PPA.

FINANCING STRUCTURE

The total project cost amounted to $4.7 million. It is financed through equity infusion of SURE Eco investors' equivalent to 67% of the project cost. The balance of 33% was through a 7-year loan that carries a 6% annual interest.

RESULTS

The project provided the following benefits:

(i)   methane capture – methane is 20 times more potent as greenhouse gas compared to CO_2,

(ii)   clean energy – avoided the use of fossil fuels,

(iii) helped address power supply deficiency of the distribution utility,

(iv)   saved SMFI of wastewater treatment cost, and

(v)   provided additional employment during construction and operation.

LESSONS

The critical factors in designing an efficient anaerobic digestion system are solid content, retention time, temperature, mixing, and sludge removal. Not all these factors were immediately addressed in the project implementation, resulting to low biogas production. The wastewater from the farm became too diluted when it changed its wastewater discharge schedule, which is why the drum thickener was added to the system. The heat exchanger was also added later to improve overall efficiency.

THE DEVELOPER

SURE Eco is a project developer focused on WtE projects using wastewater from livestock farms as feedstock and employing anaerobic digestion technology. Aside from Sumilao Farm project, it has two other similar projects with power generation capacity of 200 kW each.

KEYWORDS

waste-to-energy, anaerobic digestion, biogas, sludge, secondary waste water treatment, build-operate-transfer

FURTHER READING

CDM, UNFCCC. 2011. *Sumilao SURE Eco Energy Philippines Inc. Biogas to Energy Project.* http://cdm.unfccc.int/Projects/DB/SGS-UKL1296668897.94/view.

SURE. *Solutions Using Renewable Energy: New Horizons in Circular Economy http://www.sure.com.ph/.*

1.15   Waste to Energy Siang Phong Biogas

CONTEXT

The Greater Mekong Subregion is home to a large native starch processing industry. Cassava roots are washed and processed into starch. This starch is used in food products and is a precursor material for the manufacture of chewing gum, citric acid, and a host of other products. Farmers grow the cassava (also known as tapioca) as a cash crop. Once harvested the cassava degrades quickly. Processing needs to be carried out within 2–4 days of harvesting. An efficient and constant local supply chain is a necessity.

The processing of the starch is relatively simple. It is washed, chopped, and fermented into a soupy mix. The soupy mix is blown into a drying cyclone using heated air. The mix dries to a white powder that is bagged at the bottom of the cyclone. This bagged native starch is sold internationally as a commodity.

The energy needed for drying is typically supplied from a boiler fueled by heavy fuel oil (HFO) while electricity runs the factory equipment. Energy supply and cost are the major risk issues for any factory.

PROJECT SUMMARY

PROJECT NAME:
WtE Siang Phong Biogas

CAPITAL COST:
$3.3 million

DEVELOPER:
HD&L Co. Ltd.

PROJECT HOST:
Siang Phong Development Agriculture Co., Ltd.

GEOGRAPHICAL LOCATION:
Kampong Tbong Khmum (formerly Kampong Cham), Cambodia

TYPE OF ENERGY PROJECT:
Biogas to power and heat application

PROJECT COMPLETION YEAR:
2012

A factory producing 90 tons of starch per day requires 300 tons of unwashed cassava roots, 15,000 kWh of electricity, 3,600 liters of HFO, and 2,400 m^3 of water. Factories typically operate 16 hours per day over a 10-month growing season. In the province of Tbong Khmum, close to the border with Viet Nam, the cassava industry faced power supply challenges.

Power was sourced from Viet Nam by Electricité du Cambodge. The voltage of the power varied from 380 to 350 volts and brownouts were common. Power was provided 4 days per week on an irregular basis. This impacted production schedules and limited factory operations.

SOLUTION

The Siang Phong Development Agriculture Co Ltd (Siang Phong factory), one of the factories located in the province of Tbong Khmum, sought technical advice of HD&L Co Ltd, a local engineering company, to present a reliable and cheaper energy solution to increase their production and reduce operating costs. HD&L entered into a joint venture agreement with a company from Singapore to build a biogas plant to produce electricity. The joint venture company was named WtE Cambodia Co Ltd.

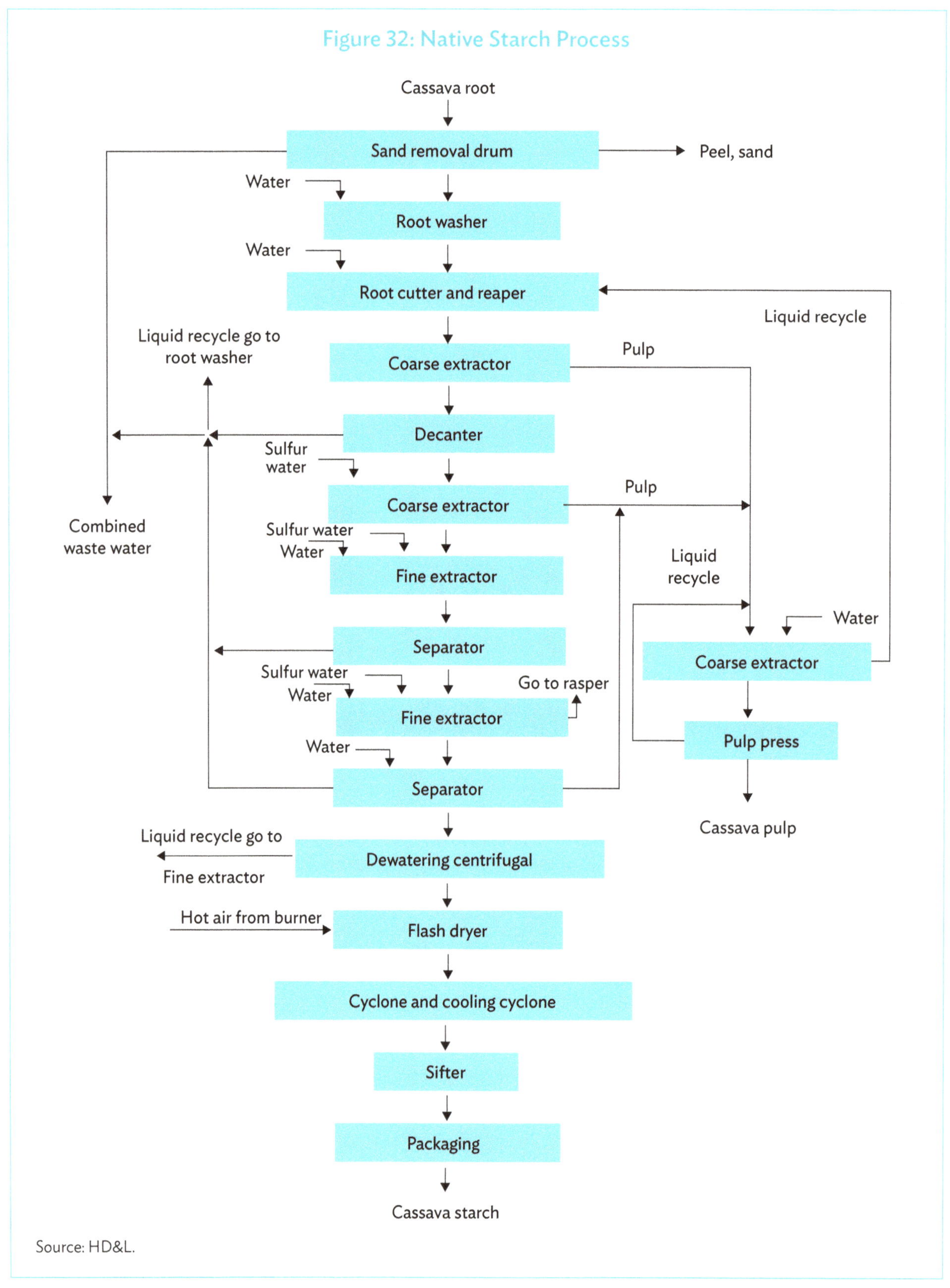

Figure 32: Native Starch Process
Cassava root
Sand removal drum
Peel, sand
Water
Root washer
Water
Root cutter and reaper
Liquid recycle
Liquid recycle go to root washer
Coarse extractor
Pulp
Decanter
Sulfur water
Combined waste water
Coarse extractor
Pulp
Sulfur water
Water
Fine extractor
Liquid recycle
Separator
Sulfur water
Water
Fine extractor
Go to rasper
Coarse extractor
Water
Water
Separator
Pulp press
Liquid recycle go to
Fine extractor
Dewatering centrifugal
Cassava pulp
Hot air from burner
Flash dryer
Cyclone and cooling cyclone
Sifter
Packaging
Cassava starch
Source: HD&L.

Siang Phong factory signed a build-own-operate-transfer (BOOT) contract with WtE Cambodia in 2007 to build a biogas plant. The BOOT contract was later transferred to WtE Siang Phong in 2008 upon the entry of other investors. The plant makes use of root wash and root cake as feedstock. The biogas generated is to be dehumidified using a condenser and biologically scrubbed of hydrogen sulfide (H_2S). Biogas is used to produce electricity and heat. The cleaned biogas is fed to a GE Jennbacher reciprocating biogas engine to produce electricity for the factory and the biogas plant itself. As an efficiency measure, the heat from the engine is being used to preheat air into the boiler. The biogas replaced the use of HFO for the boiler to produce heat. The heat is used to dry the wet starch produced using the cyclone as described in Figure 58.

The figure also shows the process where biogas is made from cassava factory effluent. The residual solids from the biogas digestion process contain nitrogen, phosphorus and potassium, an ideal fertilizer free of significant pollutants.

TECHNOLOGY

The biogas plant makes use of the Covered-in-Ground Anaerobic Reactor (CIGAR) technology, which is common for similar application in Greater Mekong Subregion area (Figure 59).

Example of CIGAR Biogas Digester. The project makes use of the Covered-in-Ground Anaerobic Reactor (CIGAR) technology to produce electricity and heat for the cassava factory (photo by HD&L).

A network of mixing pipes allows the various bacteria (methanogens and others) to collide with the nutrients contained in the factory wastewater. CIGAR™ was a trademark of the project designer, Waste Solutions Ltd. of New Zealand. The biogas production process using CIGAR technology is illustrated in Figure 60.

There is a direct link between chemical oxygen demand (COD) values and biogas production. Biogas from processing effluents is driven by the available COD. The factory effluent was estimated at 2,400 m³ daily with expected COD of 14,000 mg/l. While the COD of the effluent varies over time, additional root cake can be added to meet the overall target of 33.6 tons of COD daily. The 33.6 tons of COD is sufficient to produce 15,620 Nm³ of biogas (60% methane concentration) with pure methane content of 10,349 Nm³. The rest are CO_2 and other impurities that consist of high levels of moisture and H_2S.

The biogas engines are highly sensitive to H_2S contamination. H_2S reacts with engine oil to form plaque, which could severely affect engine operations. While boilers are less sensitive to H_2S damage, it is still good practice to remove these impurities. The flow of biogas to the boiler and the GE Jennbacher biogas engines is controlled by a program logic controller using a gas manifold.

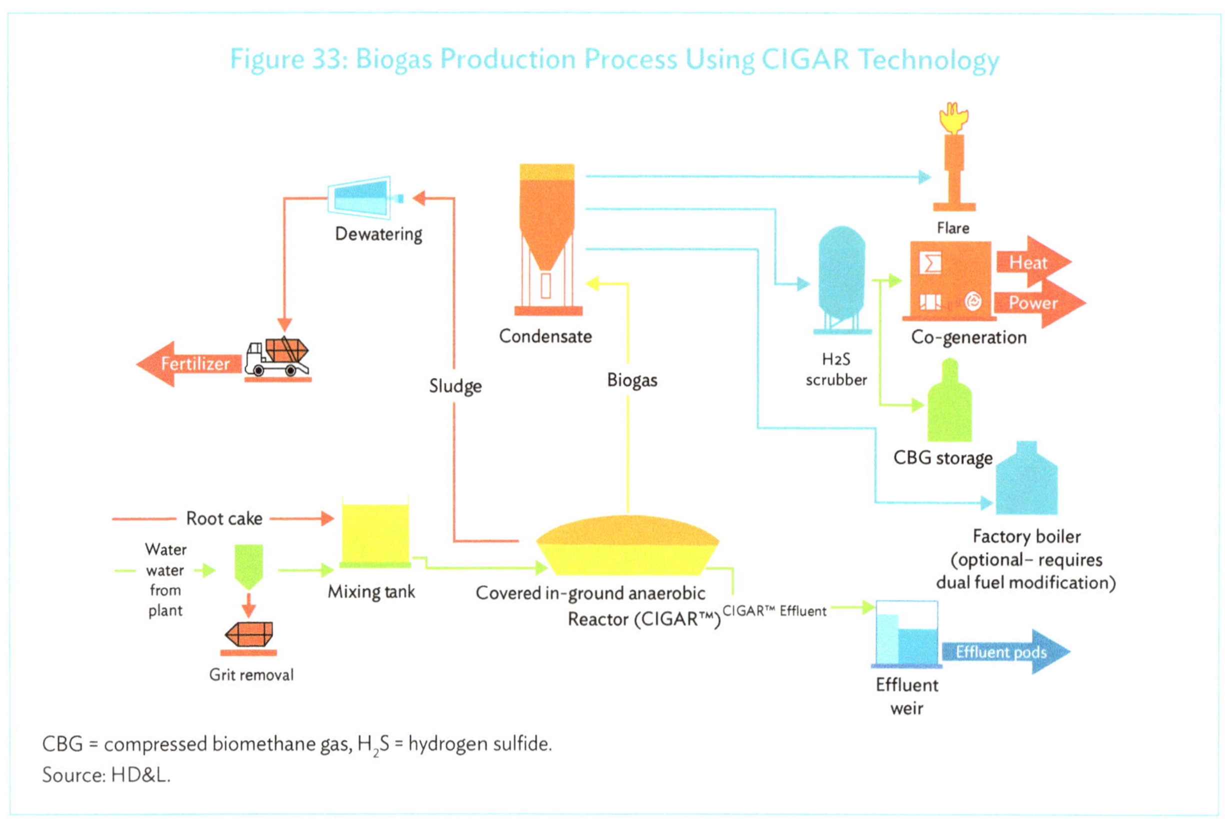

CBG = compressed biomethane gas, H_2S = hydrogen sulfide.
Source: HD&L.

Table 19: Financial Scenarios for Cassava Starch Factory Owner (Simplified)

Yearly	Scenario One–Cassava Factory (operating at 90T/hr – 55% capacity)			Scenario Two–Cassava Factory with Biogas Plant			Scenario Three Cassava Factory with Biogas Plant with increase production and root price		
	Unit	Cost $	Σ $	Unit	Cost $	Σ $	Unit	Cost $	Σ $
Inputs			4,312,364			4,098,621			6,188,793
OPEX (Days)	260	900.00	234,000	260	1,100.00	286,000	260.0	100.00	286,000
Roots (T)	77, 200	32.00	2,471,040	77,220	32.00	2,471,040	115,830.0	35.00	4,054,050
Water (m^3)	2,162,160	0.15	324,324	2,162,160	0.15	324,324	3,243,240.0	0.15	486,486
Grid (kWh)	5,000,000	0.16	815,000	0	—	—	0.0	—	—
HFO (L)	936,000	0.50	468,000	0	—	—	0.0	—	—
Power (kWh)	0	—	—	5,000,000	0.14	690,000	7,500,000.0	0.14	1,035,000
Heat (Nm^3)	0	—	—	1,363,571	0.24	327,257	1,363,572.5	0.24	327,257
Output			4,601,212			5,203,872			7,805,808
Factory waste water (m^3)	1,945,944	0.05	$97,297	1,945,944	0.05	97,297	2,918,916.0	0.05	145,946
Carbon (TCO_2e)	0	—	—	26,500	14.00	371,000	39,750.0	14 .00	556,500
Starch (T)	23,400	190.00	4,446,000	23,400	190.00	4,446,000	35,100.0	190.00	6,669,000
Biosolids (T)	11,583	5.00	57,915	11,583	25.00	289,575	17,375.0	25.00	434,363
Factory operating profit		288,848.00			1,105,251.00			1,617,015.00	
Capital cost for scenario	0	3,100,000.00	3,100,000						

— = negligible, CO_2e = carbon dioxide equivalent, HFO =heavy fuel oil, OPEX = operational expenditure, hr = hour, kWh = kilowatt-hour, m^3 = cubic meter, Nm^3 = normal cubic meter, T = tons, TCO_2e = ton of carbon dioxide equivalent.
Source: HD&L Co., Ltd.

BUSINESS MODEL

W2E Siang Phong would recover the investment in the project through the savings in the costs of electricity and HFO. Three financial scenarios are presented in Table 19.

The first scenario has a limited factory operation at 55% capacity with power supplied from the grid at $0.16/kWh. Heavy fuel prices are market driven with an assumed average cost of $0.50/liter. In this scenario, the factory makes a modest profit of $288,848 while working at slightly above half capacity.

The second scenario shows the impact of replacing HFO with biogas and biogas derived power without an increase in the cassava factory operation. This is based on the assumption that farmers are not likely to plant more roots due to the uncertainty on the sale of the roots. The second scenario shows a significant savings on the cost of energy and insulates the factory from the price volatility of electricity and HFO. An additional revenue stream of the project is the sales of carbon credits based on the 2009 price. The project qualified under an approved United Nations Framework Convention on Climate Change (UNFCCC) methodology to create carbon emission reductions (CERs). The approved methodology for the project can be found at the UNFCCC website.

The modeling price for the CERs was based on carbon price prior to the market collapse in 2017. The factory operating profit under this scenario is around $1.1 million.

The third scenario has a higher factory capacity with the assumption that farmers can secure a higher price for their roots while operational efficiencies are scaled up. More starch can be processed with the same energy price as in scenario 2. The third scenario maximized the social, environmental, and financial benefits of the project. The factory operating profit under this scenario is around $1.6 million.

FINANCING STRUCTURE

The financing for the project was sought after the BOOT contract between Siang Phong Development Agriculture Co. Ltd and the joint venture company WtE Cambodia was signed in 2008. This process took several months as it involved negotiations between WtE Siang Phong and two equity investors (Figure 61). One of the Investor 2 shareholders was an engine-leasing company. The complexity of this structure required a large amount of documentation and corporate structuring.

This level of complexity created internal processing and communication challenges. It resulted in forms of contract that were highly sophisticated for a rural enterprise. As a condition of financing, the original BOOT contract with WtE Cambodia was transferred to a new biogas asset company, WtE Siang Phong. The developers were given a small equity stake in the asset company and awarded a design-build-operate contract, mirroring the nonfinancial obligations and conditions of the BOOT contract.

The impacts of the 2009 global financial crisis, coupled with cost overruns due to a change in the import regulations and additional excavation costs, created uncertainty that delayed the project implementation by 12 months and increased the final budget to $3.3 million.

The investors sought to exit the project as it neared completion after the collapse of the carbon market. Eventually, HD&L purchased WtE Siang Phong and is now operating the biogas power plant.

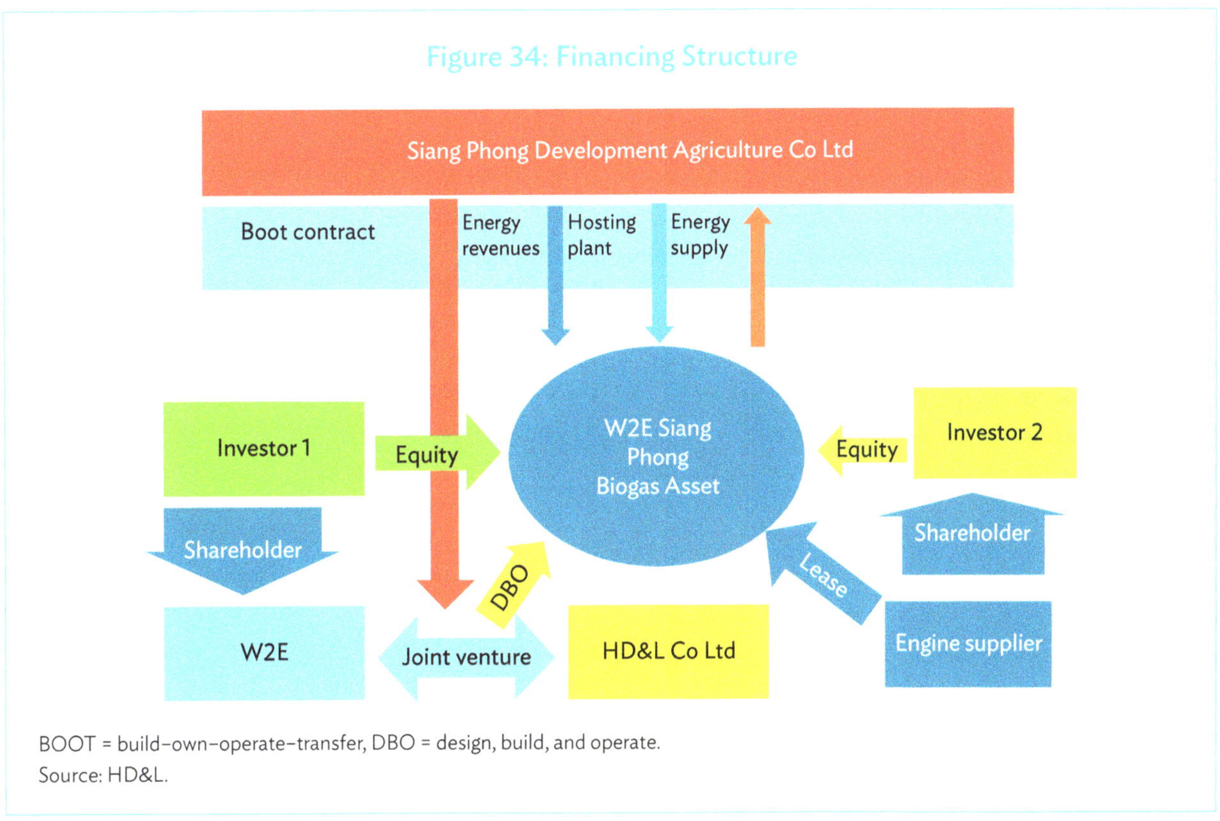

BOOT = build–own–operate–transfer, DBO = design, build, and operate.
Source: HD&L.

RESULTS

The development of the biogas plant was initially intended to provide energy security to the cassava factory.

During the development process, the strategic nature of the project became clearer. Farmers and government officials were highly supportive as there would be financial and social benefits to the local community.

The reliable and clean energy supply allowed the cassava factory to operate fully and its increased production resulted in higher incomes of farmers (Figure 62).

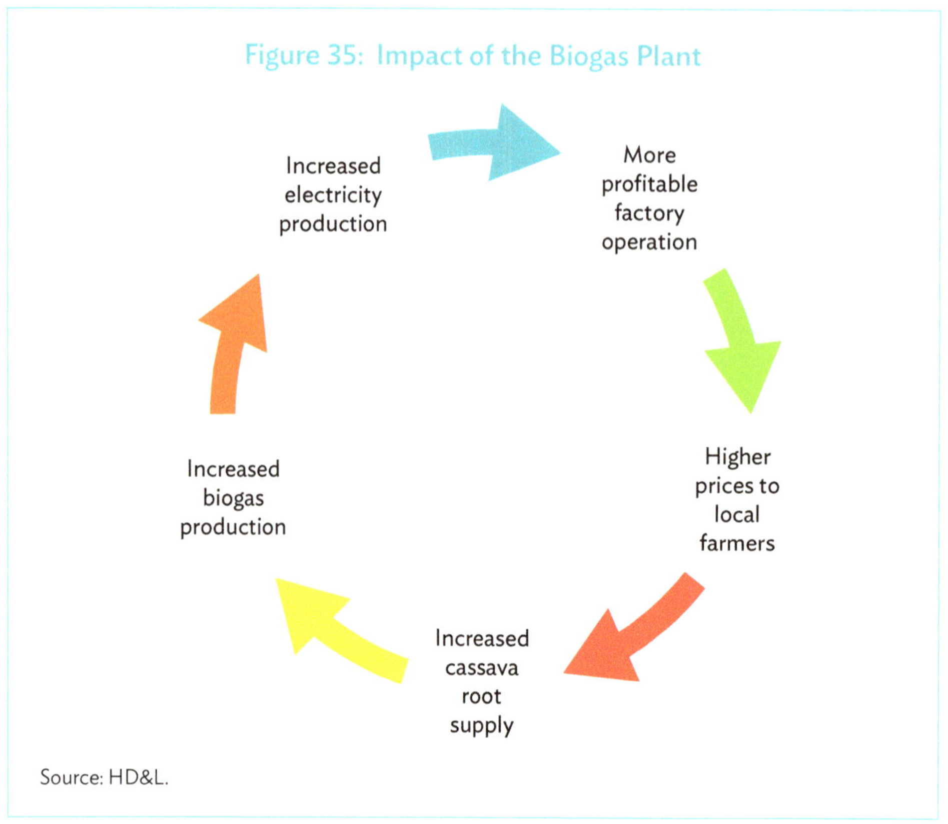

LESSONS

Smaller family-owned companies should avoid complex legal structures. Complicated reporting requirements from the different international investors and/or vendors were not appropriate for this project due to its size and nature as a rural enterprise.

Small factory owners should work with developers that have both technical and financial capability to complete the project. Financial due diligence should be made prior to signing of BOOT contract. Where possible, funding should be sourced from financial institutions that can enter into a separate contract for the management of contractor performance and delivery risks.

THE DEVELOPER

HD&L Co Ltd is an engineering service provider from Cambodia with activities in renewable energy, telecoms, technology transfer, and technical product market representation.

KEYWORDS

Covered-in-Ground Anaerobic Reactor (CIGAR), biogas, build-operate-own-transfer, chemical oxygen demand (COD), heavy fuel oil, effluents, cassava

FOR FURTHER READING

The Cambodia Daily. 2014. New Province Tbong Khmum Officially Launched. https://www.cambodiadaily.com/news/new-province-tbong-khmum-officially-launched-60322/.

Food and Agriculture Organization of the United Nations (FAO) and International Fund for Agricultural Development (IFAD). 2001. *Strategic Environmental Assessment: An Assessment of the Impact of Cassava Production and Processing on the Environment and Biodiversity.* Rome. http://www.fao.org/docrep/007/y2413e/y2413e0d.htm.

HD&L Co., Ltd. http://hdlgroups.com/index.php.

Asia Biogas Group. *Covered in Ground Anaerobic Reactor (CIGAR).* https://www.energy-xprt.com/services/covered-in-ground-anaerobic-reactor-cigar-201949.

CDM, UNFCCC. 2011. Project 4267 : W2E Siang Phong Biogas Project Cambodia?>>. Bonn: United Nations Framework Convention on Climate Change. https://cdm.unfccc.int/Projects/DB/SIRIM1292836347.34/view.

The Economist. 2012. Carbon markets - Complete Disaster in the Making. https://www.economist.com/node/21562961.

1.16   Kitroongruang Compressed Biomethane Gas Project

CONTEXT

The cassava starch industry in Thailand is a world leader in biogas production and utilization. The majority of medium- and large-size factories scale (>100 TPD starch production) have large-scale biogas plants adjoined to the factory, which treats the factory's wastewater. The biogas is mostly used as a source of heat for drying and for use in the production of electricity.

Kitroongruang Biogas Project (KIT) has been operating since 2005, utilizing wastewater from KRR Starch (the host) and selling biogas back to the host for starch drying. The project is owned by Thai Biogas, part of the Asia Biogas group. The host operating pattern of 3 days-on 3 days-off leads to irregular feeding of the biodigester, negatively affecting the process stability.

KIT typically produces around 15,000 Nm³/day biogas of which 12,000 Nm³/day is sent to the host factory, with the excess 3,000 Nm³ flared.

PROJECT SUMMARY

PROJECT NAME:

Kitroongruang Compressed Biomethane Gas (KIT-CBG) Project

CAPITAL COST:

$1 million (B33 million)

DEVELOPER:

Asia Biogas

PROJECT HOST:

KRR Starch

GEOGRAPHICAL LOCATION:

Rayong, Thailand

TYPE OF ENERGY PROJECT:

Biogas to vehicle fuel

PROJECT COMPLETION YEAR:

2018

SOLUTION

The Thai Biogas management looked at different options to utilize the excess gas. Options considered included: generation of electricity for sale to the host, generation of electricity for sale to the public utility—Provincial Electricity Authority (PEA); and by generation of compressed biomethane gas (CBG) for sale as a replacement for fossil natural gas vehicle fuel. In considering this, management also looked at the reactor performance and saw an opportunity to increase gas production significantly by taking cassava pulp as a feedstock to the digester. Cassava pulp is a solid waste stream from the cassava processing activity. Asia Biogas has pioneered its use as a biogas feedstock. As a solid feedstock, cassava pulp has the advantage over wastewater that it can be easily stored and fed to the biogas plant when required. As well as increasing gas production by increasing the amount of feed to the digester, more regular feeding is expected to improve biological performance of the reactor.

The use of excess gas to produce electricity for sale to the grid is not a feasible option in Thailand at present. In March 2018, the Minister for Energy, Siri Jirapongphan, announced that there was no plan to purchase electricity from renewable energy projects in the short to medium term.[11]

[11]   P. Wangkiat. 2018. Policy May Well Energise Alternative Power. *Bangkok Post*. 5 April. https://www.bangkokpost.com/opinion/opinion/1440954/policy-may-well-energise-alternative-power.

Using the excess gas for power generation for the factory was not feasible due to the high variation of load at the factory between operating and non-operating days. Such a project would not make use of all of the gas potential and the possibility for future expansion was limited.

The final option, producing CBG or sometimes called biomethane as a vehicle fuel, was selected as it had a number of very positive attributes:

(i)   full gas utilization,

(ii)   improved biological function through more consistent feeding,

(iii) alternative to fossil natural gas in the local vehicle fuel and/or industrial fuel market,

(iv)   potential for future expansion as market is proven, and

(v)   greater price upside as power prices get limited by solar roll out in Thailand.

TECHNOLOGY

The project generates biogas in the existing in-ground biogas reactor. Feedstock handling had to be modified to allow for the addition of cassava pulp as a feedstock. The process redesign was undertaken by Asia Biogas in-house engineering team who have pioneered cassava wastewater and cassava pulp digestion in Thailand.

PSA System Developed by Atmos Power India. The project utilized a pressure swing adsorption (PSA) system in conjunction with Atmos Power of India to increase methane capture rate (photo by Asia Biogas).

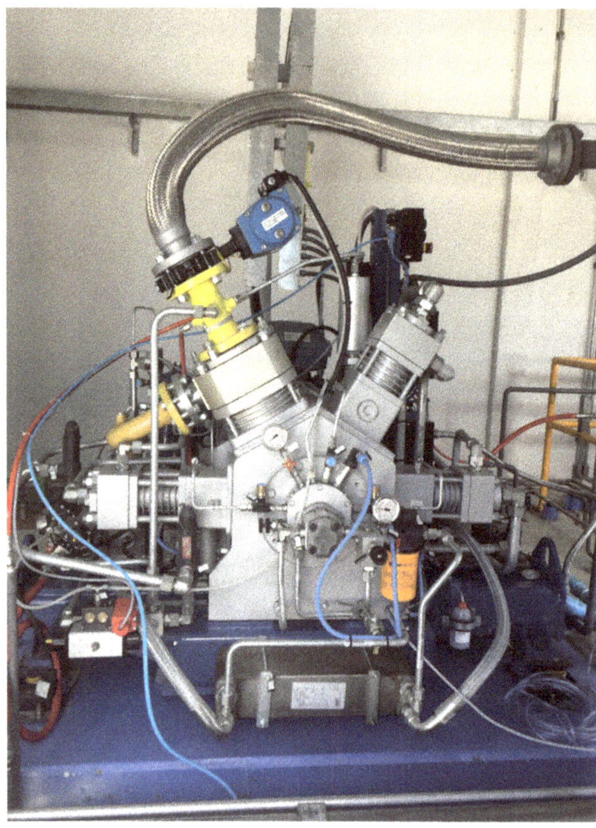

Compressor Supplied by SAFE of Italy. The compression, storage, and dispensing of the gas is undertaken using compressor and dispensing system system (photo by Asia Biogas).

Due to the relatively small scale of the project, cost control was essential and thus it was decided to opt for a low-cost option. Asia Biogas delivered a pressure swing adsorption (PSA) system in conjunction with Atmos Power of India. The PSA includes H_2S removal and moisture removal vessels before the main gas separation is undertaken in two pressure vessels (Figure 63). The two towers switch between gas separation and regeneration modes, hence the name pressure swing.

The system works by alternatively pressurizing and depressurizing a vessel containing the biogas. During the pressurization step, the carbon dioxide in the biogas adheres to a molecular sieve inside the vessel, with the methane-rich product gas passing through. When the sieve becomes saturated with carbon dioxide, a vacuum is applied to the vessel and this carbon dioxide-rich gas is directed to a methane recovery step. The methane recovery step collects further methane from the off gas and returns it to the feed gas system. The system can achieve methane concentrations of over 95%, however in Thailand local regulations only require a concentration of greater than 85%.

Once upgraded to biomethane, the gas is compressed to 250 bar and stored on-site before it is delivered to the customers' fuel tanks. Compression, storage, and dispensing of the gas is undertaken using Italian brand SAFE's compressor and dispensing system (Figure 64).[12]

---

[12]   SAFE s.pa. http://www.safegas.it/en/

BUSINESS MODEL

The product gas will be sold either as vehicle fuel to end user and/or as industrial fuel for heating and power applications.

With regard to vehicle fuel, it is intended that the project will be heavily promoted in its immediate vicinity. Despite the high quality of the gas and its environmental attributes, it is expected that to encourage end users it will be necessary to sell the gas at a discount to the prevailing PTT Public Company Limited pump price for natural gas vehicles.

As the environmental attributes are unlikely to attract a premium in the immediate vicinity, Asia Biogas is examining ways that these environmental attributes could be monetized through some form of renewable natural gas renewable electricity certificate system.

With regard to sale of the gas as an industrial fuel, a number of international clients have expressed an interest to purchase the gas with a view to using it as a means to meet their commitments to RE100[13] or other voluntary initiatives.

KIT-CBG Station Truck Refueling. The produced gas will be sold either as vehicle fuel to end user and/or as industrial fuel for heating and power applications (photo by Asia Biogas).

---

[13]   RE100 is a global, collaborative initiative of influential businesses committed to using 100% renewable electricity. This will accelerate the transformation of the global energy market and aid the transition toward a net-zero economy (https://www.theclimategroup.org/RE100).

FINANCING STRUCTURE

The project is financed by Thai Biogas in partnership with its long-term financing partner Guarantco. The project benefited from grant funding provided by both:

(i)   Government of Finland, Energy and Environment Partnership Programme of the Ministry of Foreign Affairs. (https://www.eepglobal.org/en/); and

(ii)   Government of Thailand, Department of Alternative Energy and Efficiency Compressed Biogas Programme of Ministry of Energy. (http://weben.dede.go.th/webmax/content/10-year-alternative-energy-development-plan)

RESULTS

The project has been implemented smoothly, with commissioning completed in December 2018. Changes in the host operations has reduced availability of organic material in the wastewater, requiring greater pulp feeding than expected to achieve target gas production. Alternative sources of feedstock have been identified and could be utilized in the event of any shortfall in pulp availability. Sale of the gas is relatively straightforward. The project's location in Rayong, a heavily industrialized part of Thailand with very widespread natural gas vehicle use, ensures that there is a ready market for the product CBG. Figures 65 and 66 show refueling of vehicles at Thai Biogas KIT-CBG project.

LESSONS

Biogas plants always face significant feedstock risk, which is not easily managed. In this instance, identifying alternative sources of appropriate feedstock, such as cassava pulp or third-party feedstock, help to mitigate this risk and improve functioning of the plant by stabilizing feeding rate.

The small-scale nature of the project would not normally be attractive in Thailand where there is no premium available for the product CBG. However, grant support was available and made this project feasible.

Delays in project implementation occurred as this is one of the first CBG plants in Thailand to seek a license to sell the gas to the public. As such, there have been delays in licensing as the project has at times been running ahead of the regulators. This will improve in time in Thailand, but the timing of licenses needs to be carefully considered when developing such a project.

Dispensing Gas to a Customer at Thai Biogas KIT-CBG Project. The project's location in Rayong, a part of Thailand with very widespread natural gas vehicle use, ensures that there is a ready market for the product CBG (photo by Asia Biogas).

THE DEVELOPER

Asia Biogas is the leading biogas company in the Association of Southeast Asian Nations or ASEAN, operating across the region with offices in Indonesia, Singapore, and Thailand. Asia Biogas designs, constructs, finances, and operates clean energy projects, centered on anaerobic digestion and biogas production. Asia Biogas combines energy efficiency with long-term sustainability, benefiting both businesses and the environment.

KEYWORDS

Compressed biomethane gas, pressure swing adsorption, biogas, Asia Biogas, methane, cassava pulp, starch, Thai Biogas

1.17   Rainbarrow Farm Poundbury

CONTEXT

Rainbarrow Farm at Poundbury is located on Duchy of Cornwall land outside the urban extension of Dorchester in the United Kingdom (UK). It was built as part of the Prince of Wales' sustainable community designs for the town.

With the support of the UK government, renewable energy was stimulated to create sustainable development throughout the nation. The project was among the first commercial biogas plants that included a purification plant. This plant upgrades biogas to natural gas quality and is therefore called a biogas upgrading plant. This particular plant at Rainbarrow Farm cleans gas to heat 56,000 homes and around one-fifth of the gas is converted to electricity for the plant's own use and exported to the grid to supply power to approximately 500 homes. The plant was funded by the Duchy of Cornwall.

The upgrading plant cleans the biogas from a process known as anaerobic digestion. The digestion process at the Rainbarrow Farm breaks down food waste from a nearby chocolate factory, a breakfast cereal producer, and a potato processing plant along with maize crops from local farmers. The waste is fed through a series of containers as it is digested by bacteria and the gas extracted is purified and then sent into the national grid. The plant purifies around 650 Nm³ of biogas per hour.

The plant is owned and operated by JV Energen, a joint venture between local farmers and the Duchy of Cornwall, while Prince Charles was consulted at every stage of the project. He opened the biogas upgrading plant officially in October 2012.

SOLUTION

The anaerobic digester at Rainbarrow Farm is fed with a feedstock consisting of maize, grass, potato waste, whey, and small amounts of food waste (chocolate and muesli) from local Poundbury factories. At full capacity, a biogas production of approximately 850 Nm³ per hour can be achieved. The produced biogas (which contains about 53% methane) is divided between a generator for energy generation and a biogas upgrading system for injection into the local gas grid. Roughly 200 Nm³ per hour of biogas is used to fuel a 400-kW generator. Approximately 50% of the generated energy is used on-site (to power the upgrading installation) and exported to the electricity grid, while the rest is upgraded and fed to the gas grid.

DMT Carborex® MS Biogas Upgrading Plant. The plant uses membranes in a multistage configuration to remove CO_2 to produce a purified gas stream, containing 98.4% methane (photo by DMT Environmental Technology).

Up to 650 Nm^3 per hour of biogas is led to the DMT Carborex®MS biogas upgrading plant (Figure 67), which uses membranes in a multistage configuration to remove (or polish) out CO_2. The upgraded gas leaves the Carborex®MS system as a purified gas stream, containing 98.4% methane. This purified gas stream is referred to as biomethane or bio-natural gas.

Prior to entering the local gas grid at the Southern Gas Network network entry facility, approximately 4% propane is added to the biomethane to meet gas grid specifications and to increase the energy content of the biomethane. Mercaptan is added to the biomethane to provide the distinct natural gas odor and to match the quality of existing natural gas in the grid. The biomethane flow going into the Southern Gas Network is approximately 400 Nm^3 per hour—enough gas to supply 4,000 houses in winter and 56,000 houses in summer of power and heat.

The design of the membrane separation configuration uses highly selective membranes. The system is designed to obtain low methane losses (2%), which greatly reduces the consumption and cost of adding propane. After the gas leaves the Carborex®MS system, 98% of the methane is recovered and the recovered CO_2 has a purity of 99.5%. DMT's Carborex®MS system is the only upgrading technology that also removes significant amounts of oxygen (up to 70%).

TECHNOLOGY

DMT's Carborex®MS system is a simple, cost-effective, and robust plant for biogas upgrading implemented with membranes and an energy recovery unit. The first step of the upgrading system is a preconditioning step. Removal of water and particles from the raw biogas stream takes place by condensation of the saturated incoming biogas. Depending on the amount of hydrogen sulfide (H_2S), the H_2S can be removed in large concentrations using DMT's Sulfurex® system or for smaller concentrations using activated carbon cassette filters. After removing contaminants, the biogas is compressed to provide the driving force for membrane separation. Figure 68 shows the gas desulfurization process.

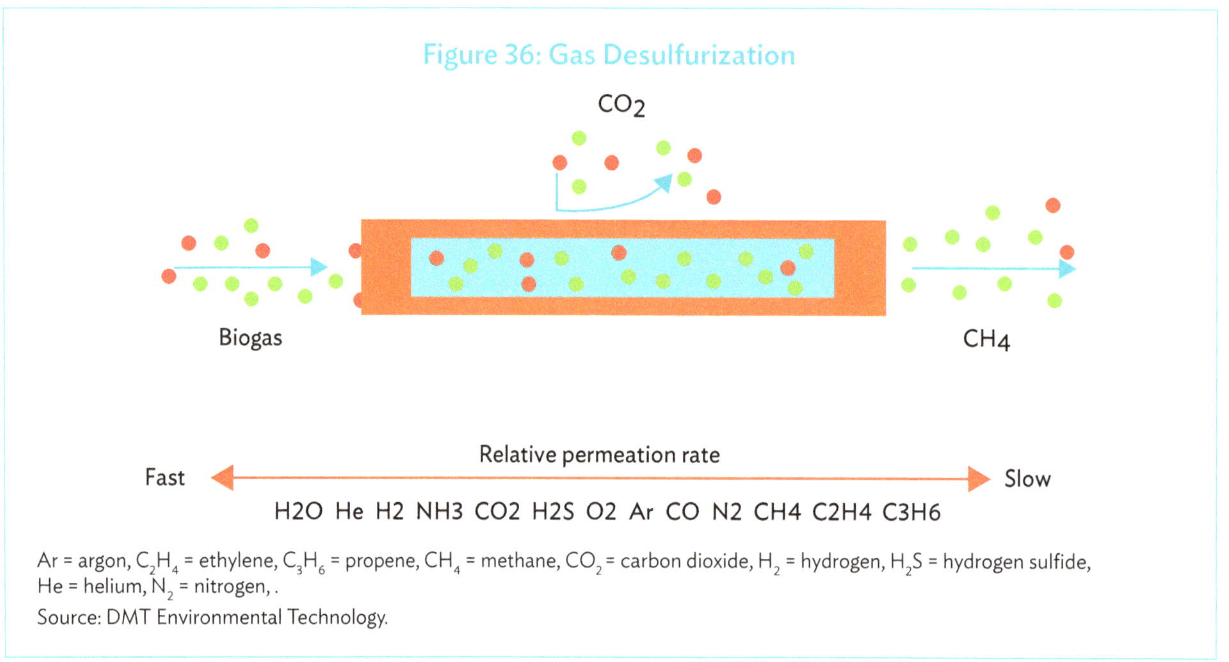

Figure 36: Gas Desulfurization

Ar = argon, C_2H_4 = ethylene, C_3H_6 = propene, CH_4 = methane, CO_2 = carbon dioxide, H_2 = hydrogen, H_2S = hydrogen sulfide, He = helium, N_2 = nitrogen, .
Source: DMT Environmental Technology.

In the membranes, CO_2 is separated from methane (CH_4). The CH_4-rich stream goes to a polishing step. The CO_2-rich gas stream goes to the energy recovery unit. Whether the specifications are met is analyzed by the quality control system. When the gas is not within specification, it will be sent to the energy recovery unit. If the quality is good, then the gas will be processed to the desired form of utilization. The schematic impression of the membrane system is provided in Figure 69.

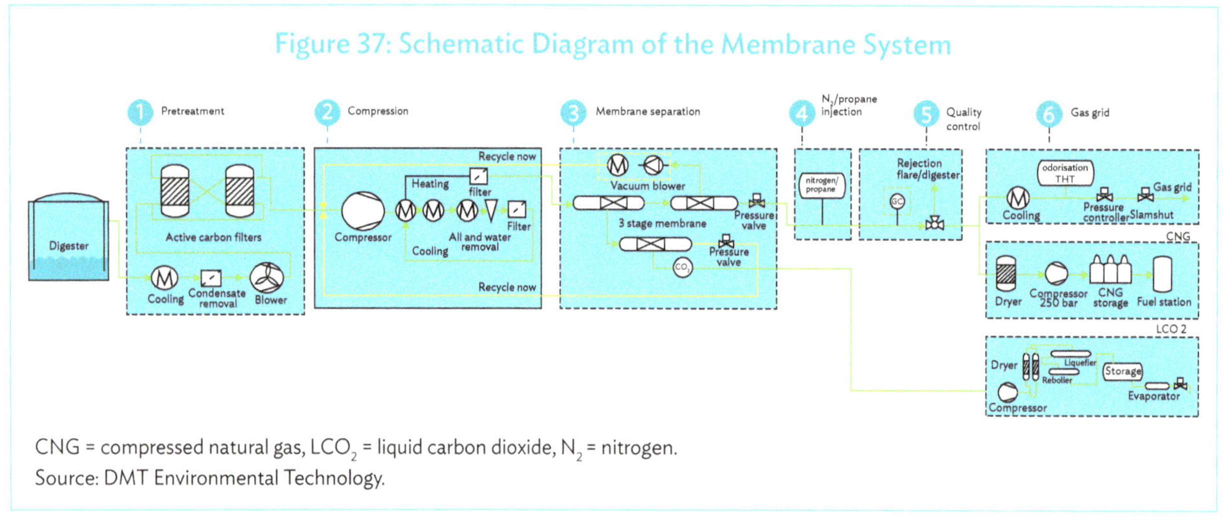

Figure 37: Schematic Diagram of the Membrane System

CNG = compressed natural gas, LCO_2 = liquid carbon dioxide, N_2 = nitrogen.
Source: DMT Environmental Technology.

Upgraded gas can be utilized in various ways using various options. The simplest is delivery to a local gas grid. Reduction valves can be used to lower the pressure of the gas so it can be used for cooking and/or heating. The gas can also be directly injected in the medium-pressure grid (6-9 barg) or compressed for the high-pressure national gas grid. For application as vehicle fuel, the gas can be even further compressed and stored as bio-CNG (220-240 bar) or even liquefied to bio-liquefied natural gas (LNG).

The bio-CNG utilization route can be easily combined with a dispenser for local use. Utilization of the treated gas directly at or nearby the production site is an important aspect for the design of the system.

BUSINESS MODEL

The national grid has identified that renewable energy gases injected to the grid could meet up to 50% of UK gas demand by 2020. Due to available incentives and environmental consciousness, upgrading biogas to feed to the national gas grid becomes an attractive proposition. In the UK, investments can benefit from a government subsidy called the renewable heat incentive, which includes support for biomethane production at all scales.

The Rainbarrow Farm is the first gas grid injection plant implemented in the UK. The farm produces biogas from maize grass and potato waste grown by local farmers as well as food wastes coming from local Poundbury factories such as chocolate and cereals. The biogas generated is used into different forms—for power and gas generation. Some portion of biogas is converted to electricity for plant use and exported to the electricity grid, while the rest is upgraded and converted into biomethane and injected into the gas grid. The gas is shipped by Barrow Shipping Ltd., which is owned by a number of participants in the Rainbow Farm project. The biomethane injected into the grid is tracked using the Green Gas Certification Scheme, which tracks biomethane through the supply chain to ensure certainty for those that buy it. The plant also produces substantial amount of fertilizer that is being used by local farmers to increase their crop and gas production.

The project uses proven technologies to ensure the technical sustainability of the project. DMT Environmental Technology supplied the Carborex®MS system for biogas upgrading and Sulfurex® system for removing large concentrations of H_2S. DMT has more than 30 years of experience and has built over 30 successful projects globally.

The plant is owned and operated by JV Energen, a joint venture between local farmers and the Duchy of Cornwall. This was built as part of the Prince of Wales' sustainable community designs for towns.

The total investment cost of this project is confidential. A general estimation of cost and performance metric for biogas upgrading to high-purity injection combined with propane injections is provided in Table 20.

Table 20: General Estimation of Cost and Performance Metric for Biogas

Figures in £m (December 2013 prices) unless otherwise stated	Capacity		
	Capacity-MW	4.0	
	Biogas capacity-Nm^3/hr	700.0	
	Biomethane capacity- Nm^3/hr*	400.0	
		£ million	$ million
CAPEX components	Development cost	1.30	1.49
	Civil works	0.85	0.97
	Waste pretreatment	2.49	2.85
	Digester waste	4.94	5.65
	Boiler	0.04	0.05
	Upgrading extra high purity + propane injection	1.35	1.55
	Injection	0.86	0.98
	Gas grid connection	0.26	0.30
	TOTAL CAPEX	12.09	13.84
OPEX components maintenance per year	Waste pretreatment	0.11	0.13
	Digester waste	0.08	0.09
	Boiler	0.00	0.00
	Upgrading	0.04	0.05
	Injection	0.04	0.05
	Gas grid connection	0.00	0.00
OPEX components– other per year	Electricity	0.26	0.30
	Propane	0.21	0.24
	Labor	0.18	0.21
	Insurance	0.10	0.22
	Landfill costs	0.13	0.15
	Landfill tax	0.42	0.48
	Digestate	0.47	0.54
	Total OPEX (before feedstock)	2.05	2.35
	Feedstock cost (£41 gate fee)	−2.11	−2.42
	Feedstock cost (£25 gate fee)	−1.29	−1.48
Subsidy (RHI) on biomethane expressed £ per MWh		97.00	111.03
EBITDA		1,453,090.00	1.663,206
Net income (EBITDA – Interest – Tax)		555.52	635.85

CAPEX = capital expenditure; EBITDA = earnings before interest, tax, depreciation, and amortization; hr = hour; MW = megawatt; MWh = megawatt-hour; Nm^3 = normal cubic meter; OPEX = operating expenditure; RHI = renewable heat incentive.
Source: DMT Environmental Technology.

FINANCING STRUCTURE

The financing of the project has been privately arranged by JV Energen, a joint venture between local farmers and the Duchy of Cornwall. The outlines of this finance structure are confidential.

RESULTS

A 400-kW combined heat and power (CHP) plant was installed on this project. Majority of the electricity generated by the CHP plant is used on-site and approximately 100 kWh is exported to the grid. The excess heat is used in the biogas digestion process. In this digestion process, the annual raw gas production is around 7.5 million Nm^3. The methane content of the gas produced in the digester is around 53%. JV Energen upgrades this gas using DMT's Carborex®MS membrane system to provide purified biomethane containing over 96% methane with a caloric value of 39.5 MJ/m^3. About 3.5 million m^3 of biomethane is exported to the grid annually.

This project represents the first commercial application of biomethane to grid. The plant has been in operation for over 6 years and has been running smoothly ever since the first m^3 was injected into the grid. Its uptime of the upgrading plant is above 98%. Further, the plant can produce 23,000 tons and 8,000 tons of solid, renewable fertilizer a year.

The Duchess of Cornwall and the local community have shown that a renewable energy approach is sustainable and profitable and has positive effects on labor and environment.

LESSONS

The first installation feeding biomethane into the gas network in the UK proved that the biomethane route is a viable and highly efficient route to generate renewable energy. Further lessons are:

(i)   Larger-scale upgrading like Poundbury can immediately supply a local community of ample renewable energy.

(ii)   Stable feedstock menu is required in order to maximize the biomethane output.

(iii)   Ease of operation is needed and can be provided by membrane technology.

Biomethane can be used as fuel (bio-CNG) for transport. It is a clean alternative for currently used fossil fuels. Biomethane is a fuel that is also cost effective and can help cities to bring down their CO_2 emissions and solve the NOx problem as public transport can use bio-CNG or even bio-LNG as fuel.

THE DEVELOPER

DMT Environmental Technology is an engineering company specializing in solutions for gas and wastewater treatment. DMT has offices globally, including in Kuala Lumpur, Malaysia.

KEYWORDS

Biomethane, Bio-CNG, anaerobic digestion, biogas, Rainbarrow Farm, Poundbury, combined heat and power, DMT Environmental Technology

FURTHER READING

Active Communications International, Inc. 2017. *Biomethane in Asia–Utilisation Routes in Different Countries.* https://www.wplgroup.com/aci/2017/06/27/biomethane-in-asia-utilisation-routes-in-different-countries/.

DMT Environmental Technology Asia. https://www.dmt-et.my/.

J. Langerak et. al. *Biogas Upgrading: Membrane Separation Takes Over—The Success Story of Poundbury Continues.* Kuala Lumpur: DMT Environmental Technology. https://docplayer.net/25142713-Biogas-upgrading-membrane-separation-takes-over-the-success-story-of-poundbury-continues.html.

Utility Week. Prince Charles Opens Groundbreaking Biogas-to-Grid Plant at Poundbury. https://utilityweek.co.uk/prince-charles-opens-groundbreaking-biogas-to-grid-plant-at-poundbury/.

BBC. 2012. Prince Charles opens Dorset food-powered biogas plant. 21 November. https://www.bbc.com/news/uk-england-dorset-20427280.

1.18   Yitong Distributed Waste-to-Energy Project

CONTEXT

Shaanxi Province has abundant coal reserves. Recent policy changes in the People's Republic of China (PRC) have resulted in smaller mines closing and a workforce refocusing on low-carbon technologies to support the Ecological Civilization, Beautiful Countryside, and Blue Sky policies.

A group of coal mine managers and engineers carried out a management buyout of their mines maintenance assets. Yitong Co. Ltd took over a large factory complex and redeployed the tools to carry out other activities.

Meanwhile, rural communities in northern PRC including Shaanxi have struggled to deal with the large amounts of straw, animal and human feces, and municipal waste. The challenge has been the distributed nature of these waste streams. Large biomass plants have provided energy and much-needed district heating in winter without addressing the other waste streams. Yitong set about designing a village-level facility to meet these demands, and to overcome the challenge for rural communities keeping warm without coal and the air pollution from its use.

PROJECT SUMMARY

PROJECT NAME:

Yitong Distributed Waste to Energy Project

CAPITAL COST:

$7 million (CNY46 million)

DEVELOPER:

Yitong Co., Ltd.

PROJECT HOST:

Yitong Co., Ltd.

GEOGRAPHICAL LOCATION:

Shaanxi Province, PRC

TYPE OF ENERGY PROJECT:

Distributed waste-to-energy factory with dry fermentation, biomass, and recycling

PROJECT COMPLETION YEAR:

2018

The Yitong team had extensive experience in materials handling. This experience allowed them to approach the problem of waste in rural communities.

SOLUTION

In 2018, Yitong executed a Changzhi county government Green Village project funded with CNY70 million (about $10 million) for supplying home heating system for seven villages with Yitong innovative biomass boiler for a period of 4 months. This project has provided heating for over 4,000 households across 400,000 square meter area. It consumed 25,000 tons of straws and produced 16,000 tons of ash.[14]

Figure 70 shows the storage yard of the existing facilities with straw and some of the fertilizer produced by the Lee Village Waste Management Facility.

---

[14] $1:CNY8.27 as of 31 December 2018 (Source: https://forex.adb.org/fx_rate/getRates).

This village currently processes 6,000 tons per 4 months of straw in the boiler; 10,000 tons per year of animal feces; and 6,000 tons per year of human feces in dry fermenter, and co-processes 20,000 tons of household waste. This is the waste stream from one village of 2,200 people. The current facility is capable of processing waste of 40,000 people.

The innovations involve the trammeling of household waste, low-cost thermophilic fermentation, 24-hour rapid fermentation for organic fertilizer, straw burner for heating and electricity supply, and homegrown gasifier design made this a remarkable achievement. The factory is highly efficient in its energy use and capital cost.

Yitong Factory Yard at Lee Village. The village can process waste stream of 2,200 people consisting of rice straw, animal feces, human feces, and household waste (photo by Yitong Co., Ltd.).

Currently, the factory operates to showcase the technology and the same will be used in this Distributed Rural Waste-to-Energy Project in Shaanxi Province. The layout of the Yitong factory is shown in Figure 71.

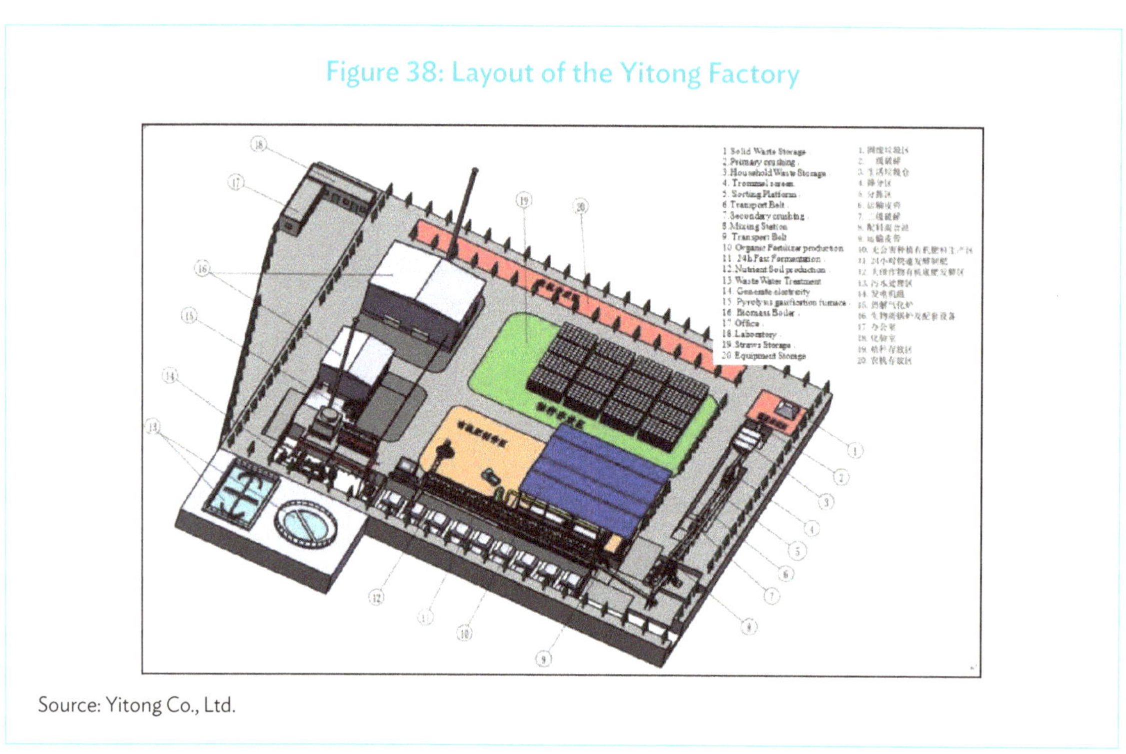

Figure 38: Layout of the Yitong Factory

Source: Yitong Co., Ltd.

TECHNOLOGY

Yitong, in collaborations with research institutes in the PRC including Tianjin University, Institute of Soil Science, Chinese Academy of Sciences, China Environmental Science Research Institute, and Shanxi Agriculture Science Institute, co-developed technologies for its One-Stop Waste Management and Processing (Figure 72).

Figure 39: Yitong Waste Processing Flow

Source: Yitong Co., Ltd.

The steps below briefly describe the processes employed by Yitong as a one-stop waste management factory. Yitong was able to design a village-level facility to generate heat and electricity and produce high-quality organic fertilizer. Yitong demonstrated the use of various technologies such as direct combustion, anaerobic fermentation, and pyrolysis.

1. **Heating and Electricity with Straws**

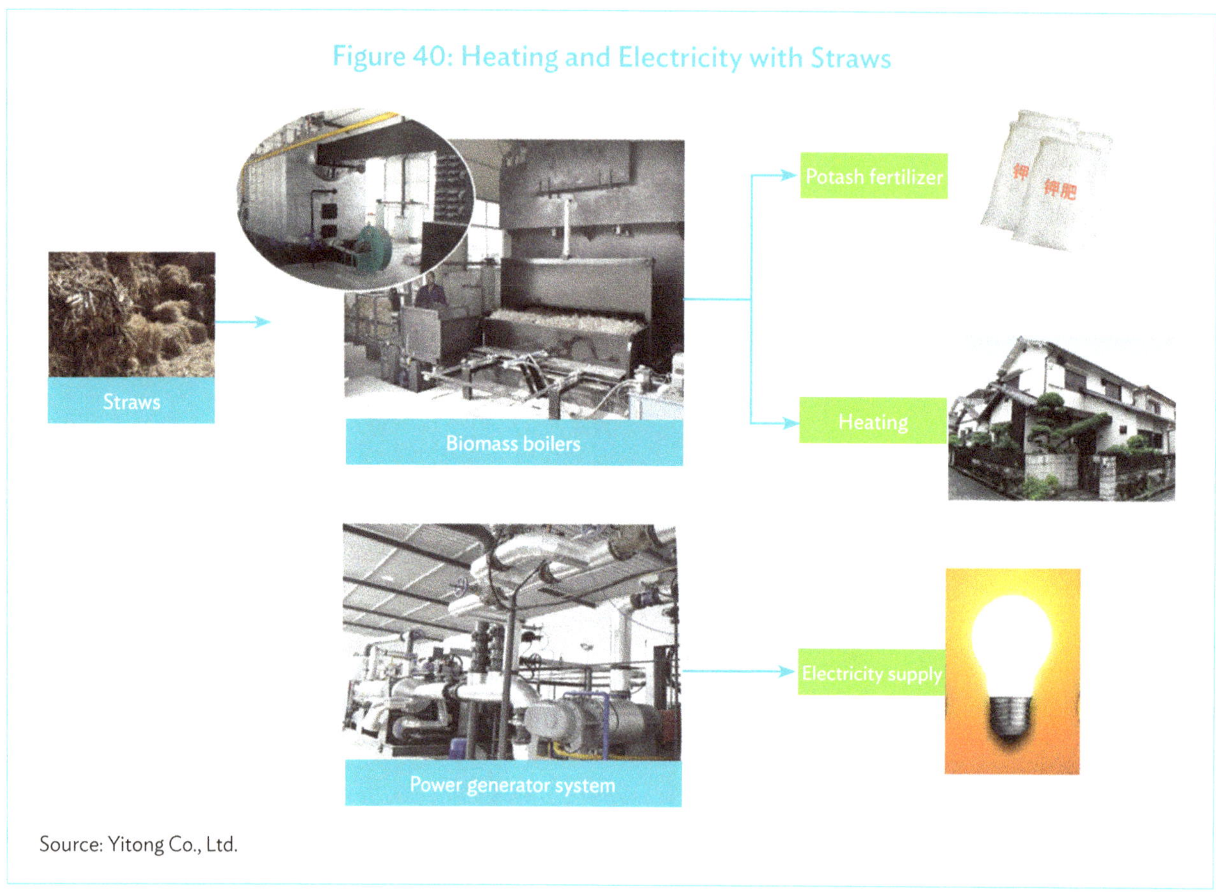

Figure 40: Heating and Electricity with Straws

Source: Yitong Co., Ltd.

Yitong has developed its own biomass boiler (integrated flue gas desulfurization and denitrification based on liquid catalytic oxidation) and power generator system (dual cycle low heat, e.g., 60°C) shown in Figure 73 above. This system has demonstrated low-cost and efficiency in supplying most needed heat during winter season and electricity the rest of the year.

2. **Waste Sorting and Crushing and System**

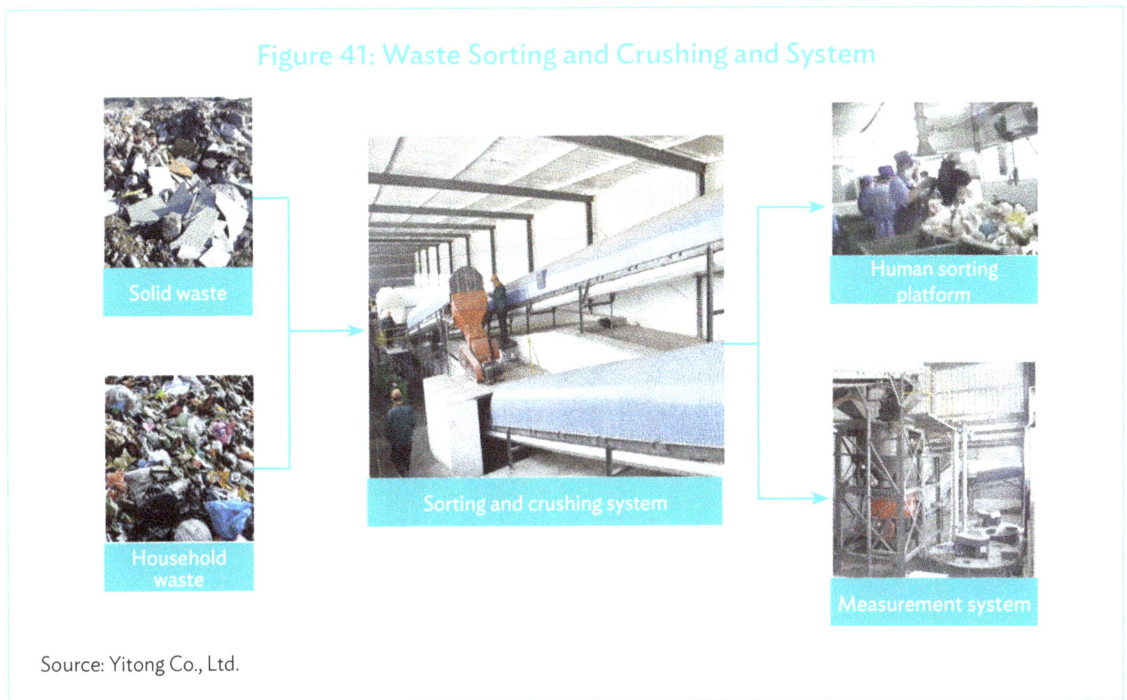

Figure 41: Waste Sorting and Crushing and System

Source: Yitong Co., Ltd.

Photos in Figure 74 show a semi-automatic waste sorting and crushing system handing both the village solid waste (construction waste) and household waste with magnetic separator, trammel screen, and sorting platform (manual), which is capable of handling 80 tons of waste a day (two 8-hour shifts operation).

3. **Anaerobic Fermentation Process**

Figure 42: Anaerobic Fermentation Process

Source: Yitong Co., Ltd.

The Yitong anaerobic fermentation process as shown in Figure 75 produces nutrient soil using solid waste powder generated from sorting and crushing processes, which is mixed with human feces with 45%–60% water with proprietary microbial fermentation agent (licensed from the Institute of Soil Science, Chinese Academy of Sciences).

4. Aerobic Fermentation Process

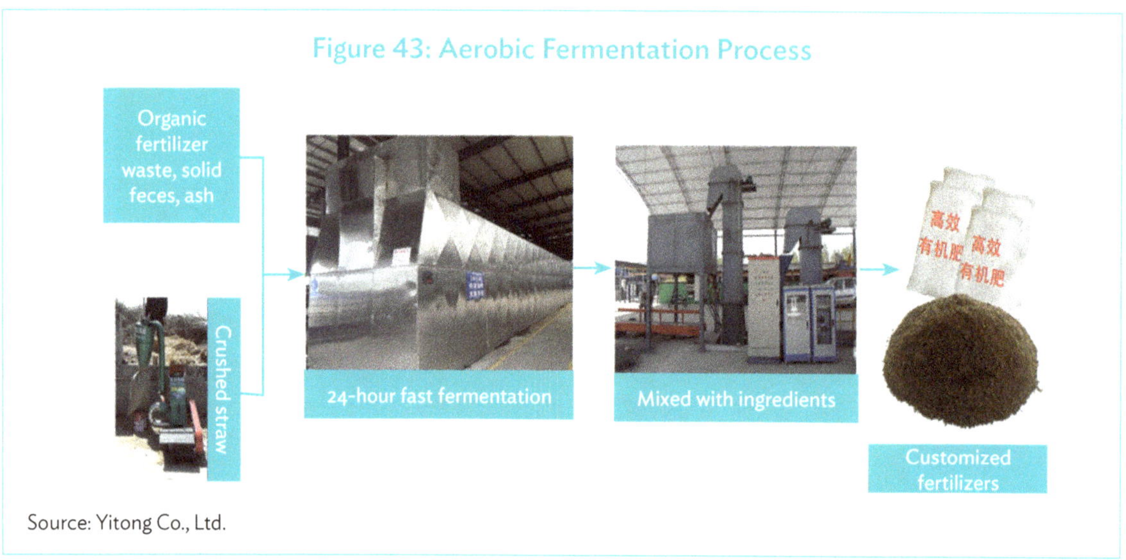

Source: Yitong Co., Ltd.

Yitong produces high-grade organic fertilizer in its special aerobic 24-hour rapid fermentation system where the sorted and crushed organic waste is mixed with dry animal feces and ash from the biomass boiler as well as straw pieces. The high-grade organic fertilizer further mixed with customized ingredients for different agricultural usage including gardening, vegetable growth, onion and garlic growth, fruits growth, etc (Figure 76)..

5. Plastics Anaerobic Digestion Process

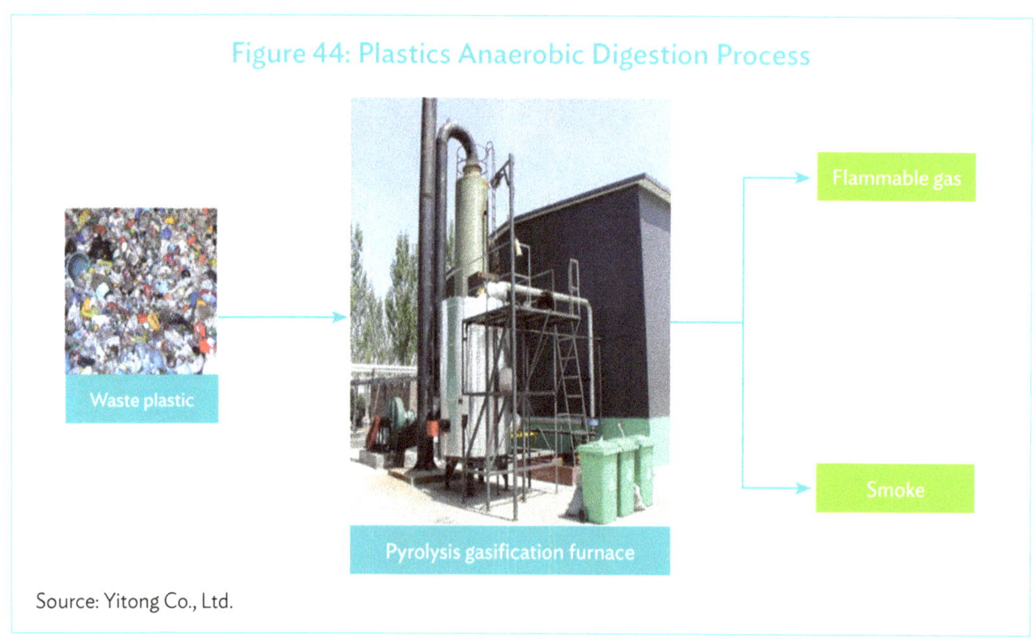

Source: Yitong Co., Ltd.

The plastic waste from the sorted and crushing platform is being treated in the pyrolysis gasification furnace producing flammable gas (with chlorine removed) and smoke, which will further scrub acidic gases, dusts, and heavy metals. The flammable gas can be further used to supply energy to the biomass boiler and the gasification furnace itself (Figure 77).

Yitong's equipment and process can be customized, designed, and manufactured according to customers' needs. The current equipment especially the semiautomated waste sorting and crushing system should be improved in its performance (with better automation) and safety standards to suit stricter environmental compliance and workers' safety. This requires further capital to produce the next generation of equipment.

BUSINESS MODEL

Yitong envisions to become a circular economy utility company. Its mission is to practice the nature-inspired agriculture production through circular business practice producing organic fertilizer and renewable energy.

Currently it has the following business areas:

(i)   heating and energy using biomass,

(ii) high-quality and customized organic fertilizer, and

(iii) agriculture products using its own fertilizer.

In 2018, Yitong revenue is about CNY120 million ($18 million), with expenses of about CNY100 million ($15 million) and with profit about CNY20 million ($3 million).

It was awarded a CNY70 million ($10.5 million) project from the Changzhi county to demonstrate green heating this winter for 7 villages and 4,000 households covering 400,000 square meters.

Table 21 provides the input of waste data, while Table 22 provides capital costs and Table 23 shows the revenue.

Table 21: Input of Waste

Rural Household Waste and Construction Waste (TPY)	Animal Feces (TPY)	Human Feces (TPY)	Straw (TPY)
25,000–30,000	15,000	7,000–10,000	6,000

TPY = ton per year.
Source: Yitong Co., Ltd.

Table 22: Capital Cost of Demonstration Project

	Machinery Equipment and Systems	Subtotal	Enclosed and Continuous Fermentation Production System	Animal Feces Pretreatment System	Subtotal	Three Boiler (16T/h)	Heating Supply Piping System	Generator System	Subtotal	Total Capital
in CNY M	6.26	3.50	2.06	1.20	3.26	6.70	14.50	12.0	33.20	46.22
in $ M	0.94	0.53	0.31	0.18	0.49	1.01	2.18	1.8	4.98	6.93

CNY = yuan, h = hr, M = million, T = ton, $ = United States dollar.
Source: Yitong Co., Ltd.

Table 23: Revenue on Demonstration Project

Item	Rural Household Waste and Construction Waste (TPY)	Nutrient Soil, N, P, K Content: 2% (TPY)	Organic Fertilizer (N, P, K content >5% Organic Matter >59%) (TPY)	Ash (4 months) (TPY)	Electricity (kVA)	Heating (4 months) (m²)	Total
Capacity	30,000.0	20,000.00	10,000	2,000	5,000,000.00	400,000.0	
Unit price (CNY)	90.0	25.00	800	1,000	0.75	12.0	
Unit price ($)	13.5	3.75	120	150	0.11	1.8	
Total revenue (CNY)	2,700,000.0	500,000.00	8,000,000	2,000,000	3,750,000.00	1,920,000.0	18,870,000
Total revenue ($)	405,000.0	75,000.00	1,200,000	300,000	300,000.00	288,000.0	2,830,500

CNY = yuan, K = potassium, kVA = kilovolt-ampere, M = million, m² = square meter, P = phosphorous, TPY = ton per year, $ = United States dollar.

Source: Yitong Co., Ltd.

FINANCING STRUCTURE

Yitong registered capital is CNY46 million ($6.9 million). The company has borrowed CNY90 million ($13.5 million) as operation capital. In 2018, Yitong reached operation profit of CNY20 million ($ 3 million).

RESULTS

Zero Waste-Yitong's waste conversion rate is 90%, the 10% includes clothes (fiber) and waste battery-based rural waste (including mixed soil plus organic waste, plastics, ceramics, metals, glass, etc.).

LESSONS

Initially, Yitong obtained organic fertilizer for the required 7 days using poor bacteria bought off the shelf. Later on it developed the 24-hours rapid fermentation system (enclosed and aerobic) through the adoption of innovative bacteria technology developed by the Institute of Soil Science, Chinese Academy of Sciences. It continues to collaborate with various research institutes to ensure access to latest innovations relating to its business.

THE DEVELOPER

Yitong is a company in the PRC involved in waste management and processing. Yitong is also an energy and heating service provider with active presence in the PRC market.

KEYWORDS

dry fermentation, biomass, Lee Village Waste Management Facility, Yitong Co. Ltd., aerobic fermentation, organic fertilizer, pyrolysis gasification, waste management

2   EMERGING TECHNOLOGIES

Many technologies are not mainstreamed in Asian Development Bank (ADB) developing member countries (DMCs). Some of these technologies are well established in other parts of the world. Others are still in the commercialization stage.

Municipalities often seek input from ADB on an unsolicited technology proposal. Very often these technologies are in forefront of technical development. The promoters are seeking locations to test the technology and develop a working track record. For ADB DMCs, this is a fraught model. A number of such projects have failed as the supply chain for waste is weak or the promoter is not able to operate the plant to desired performance criteria. This can be due to weak management, limited funds or, very commonly, internal disputes between shareholders. These are compounded by the challenges of emerging technologies.

There is a standard methodology to assess the maturity of a technology to commercialization, referred to as the technology readiness level (TRL). TRL as shown in Figure 78 provides consistency in the assessment, where TRL 1 being the idea inception stage and TRL 9 being a fully commercialization ready stage.

ADB operations and DMCs are typically most interested in TRL 8 – actual technology completed and qualified through tests and demonstrations or TRL 9 - actual technology proven through successful deployment in an operational setting. Other groups at ADB, such as Sustainable Development and Climate Change Department (SDCC), may be interested in TRL 7 – prototype ready for demonstration in an appropriate operational environment or occasionally TRL 6 – small-scale pilot projects.

Most of the solutions presented in Section 2 of the compendium are robust and commercially viable (TRL 8 or 9). Others are presented as potential pilot projects within ADB operations. The information presented is based on public domain information taken from websites and information available online as of September 2019 to determine the current estimated TRL. It is most likely many will advance in the coming years. The solutions are shown in Table 24.

Figure 45: Technology Readiness Level

Source: Innovation Canada.

Table 24: Summary of Featured Emerging Technologies

	Company Name	Feedstock	Country of Origin	Equipment Type	Output	TRL Estimate	Commercial Project
1	EcoFuel Technologies, Inc.	Plastics–PE, PVC	United States	Plastics to fuel device catalytic pyrolysis	Biofuel (diesel)	6	Suitable for pilot project within ADB operations.
2	Pyro-Kat (by Pragmatec)	Plastics–PE, PVC	Austria and Poland	Plastics to fuel device low temperature pyrolysis	Electricity and heat	8–9	Operating facilities in non–ADB countries.
3	InEnTec	Various (e.g., MSW, storm debris, industrial by-products, etc.)	United States	Plasma enhanced melter (PEM) gasification	Syngas	8–9	Several demonstration plants in the US; Taipei,China; Japan; and Malaysia.
4	Enerkem (Canada)	Various	Canada	Pressurized high-temperature process equipment	Biofuels and Renewable Chemicals	9	Enerkem Alberta Biofuels plant well established.
5	Fulcrum BioEnergy	MSW	United States	Thermochemical pressurized process equipment	Renewable synthetic crude oil	7–8	Sierra BioFuels plant in Nevada in development.
6	Cogent Energy Systems	MSW	United States	Non-oxidative high-temperature ionic gasification	Syngas	6–7	Developed and near completion of full-scale units demonstration unit.
7	Orsted	Mixed MSW, sewage	Denmark	Mechanical sorting and anaerobic digestion	Recover recyclables, biogas and refuse-derived fuel (RDF)	7	REnescience's first plant construction underway in UK.
8	Oak Ridge National Laboratory (US Department of Energy)	Effluent carbon dioxide	United States	Electrochemical process equipment	Ethanol	4	Journal articles available online.
9	Sekisui Chemical Co., Ltd & LanzaTech, Inc.	MSW	Japan	Waste-to-ethanol (distributed supply chain)	Ethanol	7–8	Pilot unit built in Japan. Suitable for replication outside Japan. Lanzatech provides technology to a number of projects in development.
10	Walbruze Waste Energy Management	Solid waste	Indonesia	Thermo-mechanical processing	RDF	7	Italian technology being localized in Indonesia.
11	Ecalox Ltd.	Waste low-grade aluminum	United Kingdom	Electrophoretic hydrogen from aluminum	Hydrogen	7	Pilot unit in the laboratory. Suitable for pilot project.

ADB = Asian Development Bank, MSW = municipal solid waste, TRL = technology readiness level, UK = United Kingdom, US = United States.

2.1   EcoFuel Technologies

OVERVIEW

EcoFuel Technologies, Inc. (EFT)[15] researches, develops, and commercializes scalable modular technologies that generate biofuel from plastic waste non-oxidatively. EFT offers multiple sizes of table-top reactor that processes and converts plastics to multiple types of biofuel.

TECHNOLOGY SUMMARY

EFT developed a proprietary nano-engineered catalysts and technology that enable gasoline, diesel, or lubricating fluids to be produced as an end product with no additional refining necessary. Plastics, specifically PE-HD(2), PE-LD(4), PP(5), and PS(6) (Figure 79) can be depolymerized into usable products, i.e., fuels using heat in the presence of catalysts developed by EFT.

TECHNOLOGY SUMMARY

COMPANY NAME

Ecofuel Technologies, Inc.

FEEDSTOCK

Plastics-PE, PVC

COUNTRY OF ORIGIN

United States

EQUIPMENT TYPE

Plastics to fuel device catalytic pyrolysis (distributed supply chain)

TECHNOLOGY STATUS (2018)

Available – recently commercialized

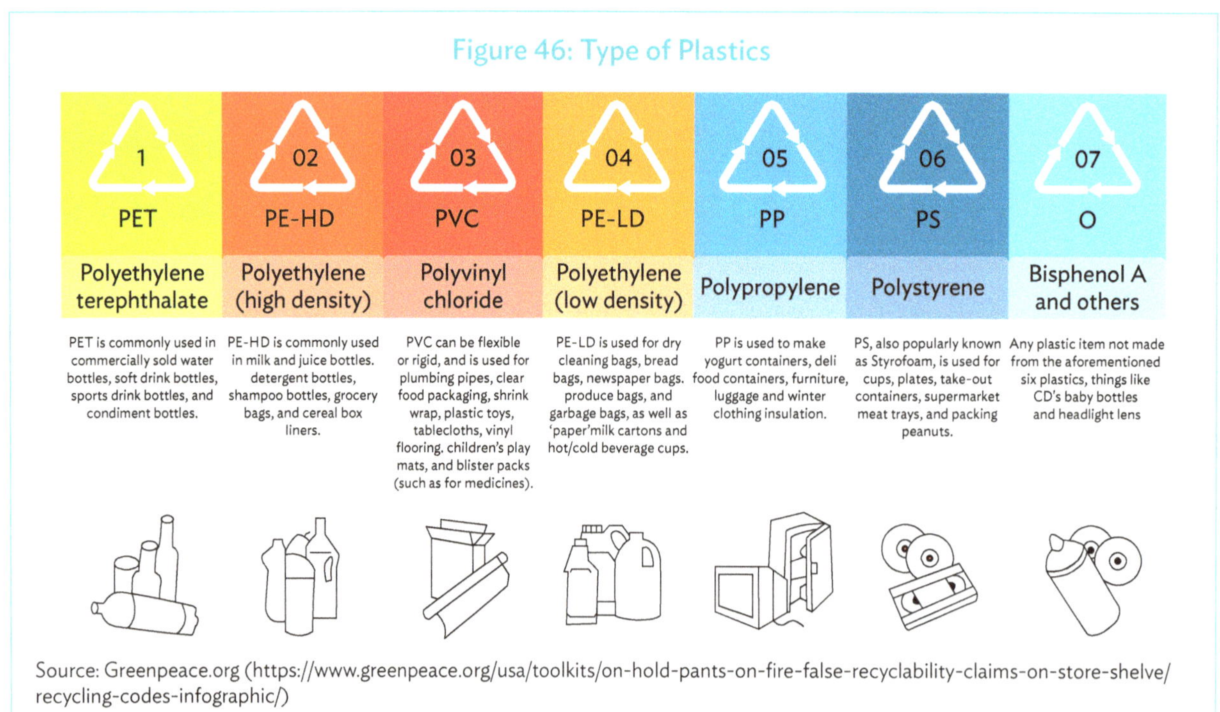

Source: Greenpeace.org (https://www.greenpeace.org/usa/toolkits/on-hold-pants-on-fire-false-recyclability-claims-on-store-shelve/recycling-codes-infographic/)

---

[15]   EcoFuel Technologies. Renewables and Environment. Michigan. www.ecofueltechnology.com.

Typically, this is achieved at high temperatures, but EFT's lower temperature (350°C–450°C) catalytic process converts plastics to fuel at a lower cost with yields as much as 80%. This could be considered a lower temperature catalytic pyrolysis.

By-product gases can be burned to supply the heat for the process, while the char remains at about 5% (by mass) may require further processing before use or disposal in a landfill. Char could also have market for asphalt manufacturers.

EFT's technology is said to tolerate impurities to a certain extent allowing processing of commingled plastic. As separation and cleaning of different plastic types are not required, preparation costs and labor resource requirements are minimized. The technology is portable and can be transported to where the plastics are located allowing the conversion of plastics to fuel (PTF) on-site. EFT's PTF units are available in sizes capable of handling 200 to 10,000 pounds of plastics a day and can be scaled as needed for up to 900 tons (2 million pounds) of plastic per day (Figure 80 and Figure 81).

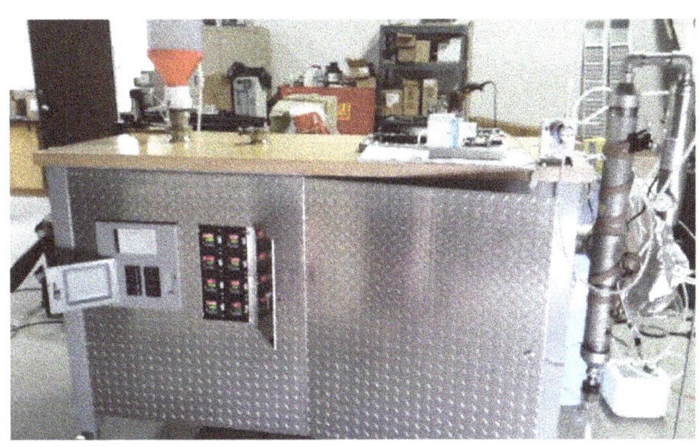

Smallest Unit Ecofuel PTF200 with Fractionator. The technology is portable and can be transported to where the plastics are located allowing the conversion of plastics to fuel on-site (photo by Ecofuel Technologies).

Source: Ecofuel Technologies, Inc.

2.2   Pragmatec & Pyro-Kat Environmental Technologies GmbH

OVERVIEW

Pyro-Kat, which was developed by Pragmatec & Pyro-Kat Environmental Technologies GmbH,[16] is essentially a pyrolysis technology. It involves disposal of hazardous and nonhazardous organic waste, based on process of low temperature quasi-pyrolysis (mineralization).

TECHNOLOGY SUMMARY

Traditional pyrolysis requires temperatures at 800°C–1100°C resulting in the formation of liquid products such as tar due to the decomposition as well as physical and chemical changes of the pyrolyzed material. However, the Pyro-Kat technology involves mineralization at low temperature (up to 500°C) quasi-pyrolysis. Pyro-Kat's process plant uses what appears to be a standard industrial process equipment. Figure 82 shows layout and typical equipment in Pyro-Kat process plant.

TECHNOLOGY SUMMARY

COMPANY NAME

Pyro-Kat (by Pragmatec)

FEEDSTOCK

Plastics-PE, PVC

COUNTRY OF ORIGIN

Austria and Poland

EQUIPMENT TYPE

Plastics to fuel device low temperature pyrolysis (distributed supply chain)

TECHNOLOGY STATUS (2018)

Available – operational

Layout and Typical Equipment in Pyro-Kat Process Plant. The Pyro-Kat technology involves disposal of hazardous and nonhazardous organic waste, based on process of low temperature quasi-pyrolysis (mineralization) (photo by Pyro-Kat).

---

[16]   Pragmatec. *Pyro-Kat Environmental Technologies*. Vienna. www.pragmatec.at/en/pyro-kat-environmental-technology.

The output of the technology is the generation of electricity and heat. It emits combustible gases containing CO and C_xH_y, which are subsequently oxidized/reduced to H_2O and CO_2 while generating harnessable useful heat. Pragmatec claimed that Pyro-Kat's CO_2 emission is 20 times smaller than emission from incineration plant. The post-processing waste is inert mineralized inorganics (calcium oxide [CAO], aluminum oxide [Al203], silicon oxide [SiO2], iron oxide [FE203]), and unoxidized metal/gas) with minute quantities of hazardous metals. Pyro-Kat's emission and waste are suitable within the European Union limits. Organic carbon content is <1% weight. Another feature of the technology is the reduction in weight and size. Waste mass reduction is 20–400 fold and volume reduction is 15–100 fold. Several operating plants are referred since 1980. The technology has not been deployed in Asia.

2.3   InEnTec

OVERVIEW

InEnTec[17] has patented a plasma enhanced melter (PEM), a system that takes waste material and rearranges the molecules into basic building blocks to make other commercial products.

TECHNOLOGY SUMMARY

The technology builds on $300 million of earlier US Department of Energy (US DOE)-sponsored research, which confirmed the attractiveness of plasma-arc waste treatment for a variety of waste types including MSW, storm debris, industrial by-products, etc. PEM merges two different technologies—plasma technology and glass-melter technology on which multiple plasma electrodes provide radiant heating, and additional submerged electrodes provide resistive heating with good process control, to produce syngas.

TECHNOLOGY SUMMARY

COMPANY NAME

InEnTec, Inc.

FEEDSTOCK

Various (e.g., municipal solid waste, storm debris, industrial by-products, hazardous materials, others)

COUNTRY OF ORIGIN

United States

EQUIPMENT TYPE

Plasma gasification (distributed supply chain)

TECHNOLOGY STATUS (2018)

Available – operational

The PEM system takes any type of waste material (household trash, industrial hazardous and nonhazardous waste, medical waste). It presents a dual revenue stream since it produces energy as well as other products that can be sold to both energy or manufacturing companies.

InEnTec Plant in Arlington, Oregon—Model G100P. The plant in Oregon converts municipal solid waste into ultra-clean syngas, for further production of renewable hydrogen (photo by InEnTec).

---

17   InEnTec. *Clean Planet Technologies*. Richland, WA. www.inentec.com.

InEnTec opened its Technology Center in Richland, Washington in 1996, where development efforts led to commercialization and deployment of PEM systems. PEM is now a proven technology and InEnTec deployed 12 PEM systems. PEM systems are available in different sizes, ranging from G30, which is a fully contained and self-sufficient transportable PEM system on two flat-bed trailers (Figure 84) to a much larger G500. The photo in Figure 83 shows the G100P model installed in Arlington, Oregon. The list of projects is available in the company website: www.inentec.com/pem-facilities.

InEnTec Transportable Model G30. This model is a fully contained and self-sufficient transportable plasma enhanced melter (PEM) system on two flat-bed trailers (photo by InEnTec).

2.4   Enerkem (Canada)

OVERVIEW

Enerkem[18] produces clean fuels and green chemicals from waste to replace fossil fuels. Enerkem proposes a non-oxidative thermal gasification technology that converts waste feedstock into methanol, ethanol, or other renewable chemicals.

TECHNOLOGY SUMMARY

Enerkem's process is environment friendly, requiring relatively low temperatures and pressures, thereby reducing energy requirements and costs. The technology follows a four-step thermochemical process: feedstock preparation, gasification, cleaning and conditioning of syngas, and catalytic synthesis (Figure 85).

TECHNOLOGY SUMMARY

COMPANY NAME

Enerkem

FEEDSTOCK

Various

COUNTRY OF ORIGIN

Canada

EQUIPMENT TYPE

Pressurized high-temperature process equipment (distributed supply chain)

TECHNOLOGY STATUS (2018)

Available – operational

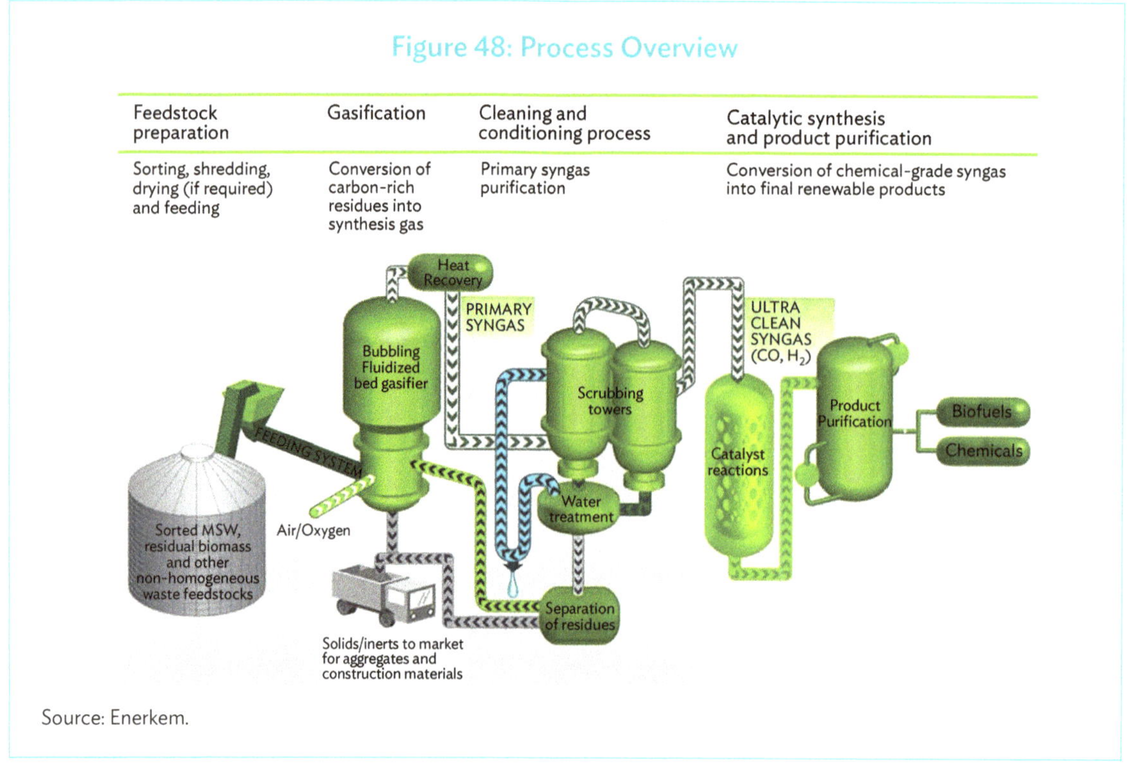

Figure 48: Process Overview

Source: Enerkem.

---

18   Enerkem. *Setting a New Sustainable Standard in Waste Management around the World.* https://enerkem.com.

A number of different feedstocks, from solid waste coming from several municipalities to dozens of other types of residues, were tested and validated using Enerkem's technology. Through thermochemical process, the carbon contained in nonrecyclable waste was recycled within 5 minutes. The process converts first this carbon into a pure synthesis gas (also called syngas), which is then turned into biofuels and chemicals, using commercially available catalysts. Syngas is converted into methanol, ethanol, or other renewable chemicals. Methanol is an important chemical component for the production of secondary chemicals, such as olefins, acrylic acid, n-Propanol, and n-Butanol, which can then be used to form a variety of everyday products.

Enerkem is an established proprietary technology that was rigorously scaled up from pilot to demonstration to commercial stage over 10 years. The company provides fully fabricated modular equipment and handles equipment assembly on-site.

Enerkem develops and delivers bio-refineries in North America and globally, based on a modular and standardized manufacturing approach. It is involved in several projects to provide a sustainable alternative solution for nonrecyclable wastes, converting waste plastics and other mixed wastes into new raw materials, e.g., green methanol, resulting in significant CO_2 emissions reduction. Figure 86 shows the Enerkem plant in Alberta, Canada.

A waste-to-chemical facility is to be developed in Rotterdam to provide a sustainable solution for nonrecyclable wastes converting waste plastics and other mixed wastes into new raw materials. As part of a consortium, Enerkem will be the technology provider, lead contractor, as well as an equity partner in the project. The project will convert up to 360,000 tons per annum of waste into 220,000 tons (270 million liters) of green methanol. This represents the total annual waste generated of more than 700,000 households and realizing a CO_2 emission savings of about 300,000 tons.[19]

Enerkem Alberta Biofuels. The facility is designed to turn household garbage into biofuels and renewable chemicals to reduce greenhouse gas emissions (photo by Enerkem).

---

[19]   Enerkem. *Waste Management World*. https://waste-management-world.com/tag/Enerkem.

2.5   Fulcrum BioEnergy

OVERVIEW

Fulcrum[20] is engaged in making low-carbon transportation fuels from household garbage. It developed a non-oxidative gasification and thermochemical technology that converts MSW into low-carbon renewable transportation fuels including jet fuel and diesel.

TECHNOLOGY SUMMARY

The process starts with the gasification of the organic material in the MSW feedstock to a synthesis gas (syngas), which is composed of carbon monoxide, hydrogen, and carbon dioxide. The syngas is then purified and processed using Fischer-Tropsch process to produce a syncrude product, which is then upgraded to jet fuel or diesel. The heat generated during the process produced electricity to help power each plant, which will limit additional strain to the grid as well as reduce the generation of harmful emissions. The technology is modular and scalable from a 10-million gallon to a 60-million gallon per year plant.

The company has one plant under construction in Storey County, Nevada (Figure 87). The feedstock processing facility was completed in 2016, and the bio-refinery is expected to be completed in 2020. A strategic investment by United Airlines and partnerships with United Airlines, Cathay Pacific, BP, and the US Navy and Air Force are helping to accelerate their development program and fuel delivery to the market.

Their process has been reviewed by several third parties including independent engineers, the US Department of Defense and the US Department of Agriculture.

Fulcrum has entered into agreements providing long-term access to competitively priced MSW feedstock totaling about 4% of the garbage landfilled annually in the US. Currently, the company is developing projects that are able to produce hundreds of millions of gallons of low-cost, low-carbon transportation fuel across North America. Fulcrum projects intend to be constructed with:

(i)   secured feedstock (100%);

(ii)   long-term offtake agreement;

(iii)   engineering, procurement, and construction contract guaranteeing the cost and performance of the plant; and

(iv)   investment-grade technology insurance to guarantee performance of the plant.

TECHNOLOGY SUMMARY

COMPANY NAME:

Fulcrum BioEnergy

FEEDSTOCK:

Municipal solid waste

COUNTRY OF ORIGIN:

United States

EQUIPMENT TYPE:

Thermochemical pressurized process equipment (Distributed supply chain)

TECHNOLOGY STATUS (2018):

Tested but not yet operational

---

20   Fulcrum BioEnergy. fulcrum-bioenergy.com.

Fulcrum FPF and Bio-Refinery Under Construction. – The facility will be the first commercial-scale plant converting a municipal solid waste feedstock into a low-carbon, renewable transportation fuel product.

In 2015, United Airlines announced a $30 million equity investment in Fulcrum BioEnergy. Fulcrum's renewable jet fuel is expected to provide 80% reduction in life cycle carbon emissions when compared to conventional jet fuel. United Airlines has negotiated a long-term supply agreement with Fulcrum to have the opportunity to purchase at least 90 million gallons of sustainable aviation fuel a year, for a minimum period of 10 years at a cost competitive with conventional jet fuel.[21]

[21] *Biofuels Digest*. 2015. United Airlines Invests $30M in Fulcrum BioEnergy; Inks $1.5B+ in Aviation Biofuels Contracts. https://www.biofuelsdigest.com/bdigest/2015/06/30/united-airlines-invests-30m-in-fulcrum-bioenergy-inks-1-5b-in-aviation-biofuels-contracts/. Also appeared in Insidewaste. 2015. https://www.insidewaste.com.au/general/news/1002437/united-airlines-invests-usd30m-msw-biofuel.

2.6   Cogent Energy Systems

OVERVIEW

Cogent Energy Systems[22] develops a proprietary technology called HelioStorm, which is essentially a non-oxidative ionic gasification technology that converts MSW to synthesis gas (syngas) to fuel a quick ramping electricity generator.

TECHNOLOGY SUMMARY

Globally, there are millions of small-scale waste producers who lack a viable way to process their local waste on-site—much less turn it into valuable products like electricity, fuels, or chemicals. The proprietary ionic gasification process HelioStorm gasifier converts MSW to syngas, to fuel a quick ramping electricity generator. Thereby, communities and enterprises, particularly small and remote ones, can eliminate their waste stream on-site while generating surplus energy that they can use or sell.

TECHNOLOGY SUMMARY

COMPANY NAME:

Cogent Energy Systems

FEEDSTOCK:

Municipal solid waste

COUNTRY OF ORIGIN:

United States

EQUIPMENT TYPE:

Non-oxidative high-temperature ionic gasification (Distributed supply chain)

TECHNOLOGY STATUS (2018):

Under development

The technology involves the direct-contact processing of waste inside an active plasma field at temperatures of 3,000°C–10,000°C, i.e., 5–15 times hotter than other conversion processes such as incineration, traditional gasification, and pyrolysis. Carbon vaporizes at these temperatures, breaking down completely into gaseous carbon atoms. Once immersed in the ionic gasification zone, waste spontaneously breaks all the way down to individual atoms, yielding complete single-step conversion to clean syngas that contains virtually no by-products, long-chain hydrocarbons, toxins, or harmful elements (Figure 88).

HelioStorm only requires a few thousand square feet of space, and power up in a few minutes. One HelioStorm-based WtE system can convert 4 tons of waste per day into about 3 MWh of usable surplus electricity—enough to power more than 100 households in the US. Its ionic gasification technology allows for small-scale WtE applications (economically viable at <5 TPD as opposed to only large facilities so far), which can stabilize decentralized micro-grids with dispatchable power. The result of the process is a clean, high-energy syngas that can be used to make many valuable end products including electricity, hydrogen, liquid fuels, and chemical precursors, without any furans, dioxins, or similar pollutants, and the oxygen-starved process prevents the formation of nitrogen and sulfur oxides.[23]

---

22   Cogent Energy Systems. www.cogentenergysystems.com.
23   Waste Management World. 2017. *In-Depth: Ionic Gasifier Opens Up Door to Small-Scale Waste-to-Energy*. July. https://waste-management-world.com/a/in-depth-ionic-gasifier-opens-up-door-to-small-scale-waste-to-energy.

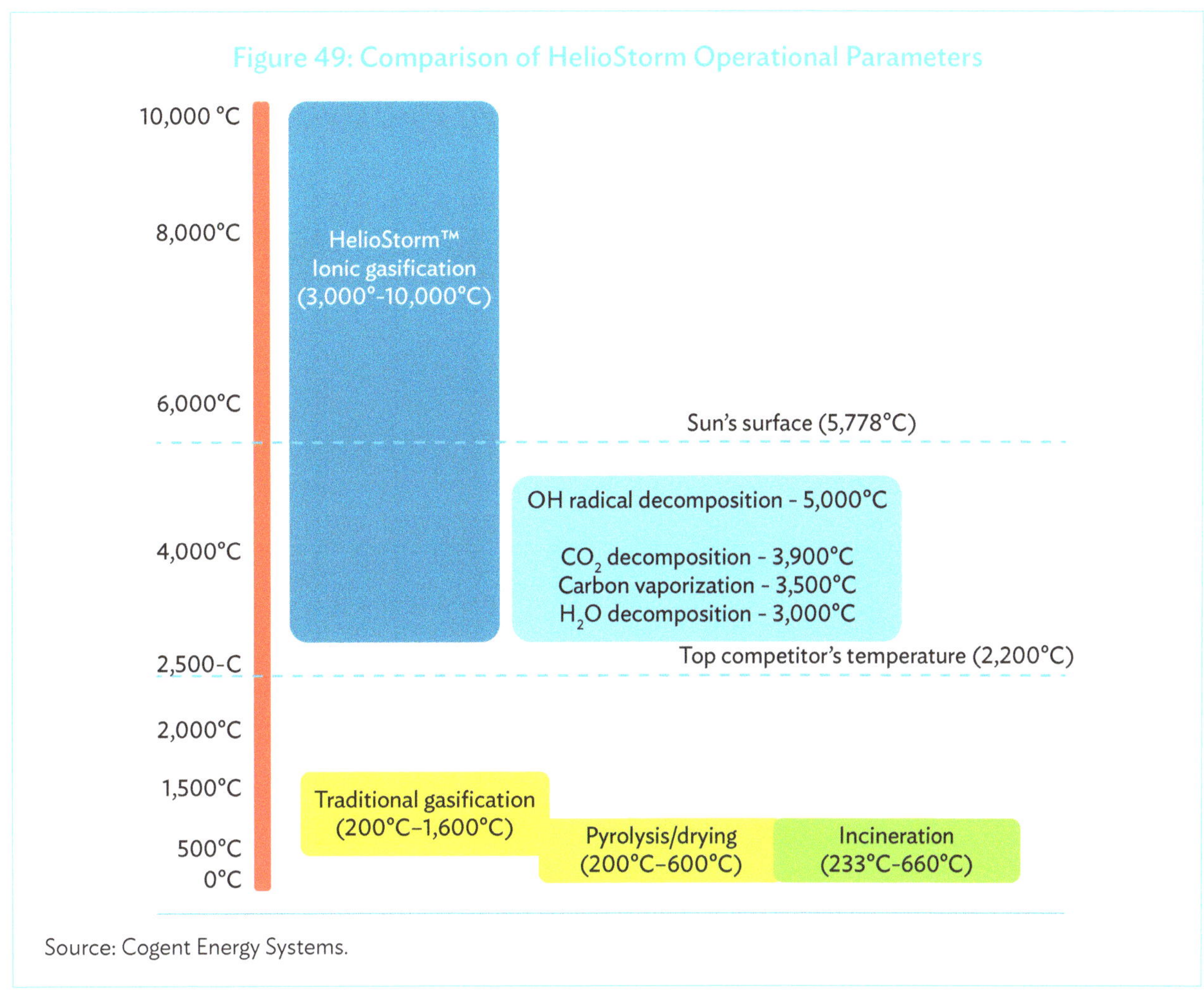

Source: Cogent Energy Systems.

Since 2012, the company has been awarded a succession of grants from the US Navy, the National Renewable Energy Laboratory, and the Idaho National Laboratory. In partnership with these organizations and Creare, Cogent has developed and demonstrated two full-scale WtE gasifiers at its Idaho Falls facility, with a complete end-to-end commercial demonstration system scheduled to come online by 2019.[24]

The technology is still under development and currently pending commercial demonstration.

[24]   P. Kong. Cogent Energy Systems. Federal Laboratory Consortium for Technology Transfer. 2020. https://federallabs.org/successes/awards/awards-gallery/2019/cogent-energy-systems

2.7   Orsted (formerly DONG Energy)

OVERVIEW

Orsted[25] is the largest energy company in Denmark. It changed its name from Danish Oil and Gas (DONG) Energy to Orsted in 2017 as it exited the oil and gas business to focus on renewables. Orsted developed REnescience technology, which is essentially an enzymatic anaerobic digestion process that uses enzymes to recover energy from mixed MSW and improve the anaerobic process.

TECHNOLOGY SUMMARY

REnescience technology uses enzymes to recover recyclables, biogas, and refuse-derived fuel (RDF) from unsorted MSW. REnescience separates household waste into recyclables by using enzymes, mechanical sorting, recycled water, and anaerobic digestion. It then liquefies the organics from the waste and turns it into green energy. The process is being adapted to treat municipal effluent sewage. The first commercial plant is designed to treat 144,000 tons per year of municipal waste and have a capacity of 6.3 MWe derived from processing biogas produced at the facility.

TECHNOLOGY SUMMARY	
COMPANY NAME:	Orsted
FEEDSTOCK:	Mixed municipal solid waste, sewage
COUNTRY OF ORIGIN:	Denmark
EQUIPMENT TYPE:	Standard process equipment (Distributed supply chain)
TECHNOLOGY STATUS (2018):	Under construction/Pending commercial operation

As of July 2018, Orsted was developing three major REnescience technology-based plants but it has struggled to get any of the facilities off the ground, due to legal and other operational issues. Construction is still in progress on Orsted's first full-scale REnescience plant in Northwich, England, which uses enzymes to recover energy from mixed MSW and improve the anaerobic process, and is expected to be operational by first half of 2019.[26] Orsted is collaborating with Novozymes to supply the enzymes. If proven commercially, this technology has a good potential to become a competitive answer to the global MSW issue.

---

25   Orsted. https://orsted.com/en/About-us.

26   J. Doherty. 2019. 'Mechanical Challenges' Delay Ørsted Bioliquid Plant. *Environment Media Group*. 31 January. https://www.letsrecycle.com/news/latest-news/mechanical-challenges-delay-orsted-bioliquid-plant/.

2.8   Oak Ridge National Laboratory

OVERVIEW

Oak Ridge National Laboratory[27] developed an electrochemical process that converts CO_2 to ethanol fuel through nano-spike catalysts. This is done to consume excess electricity, and the produced fuel can then be stored and used when needed.

TECHNOLOGY SUMMARY

The process involves nanofabrication and catalysis science, using an electrochemical process that produces tiny spikes of carbon and copper to transform GHG into biofuel. The catalyst consists of copper, nitrogen, and carbon, and the applied voltage enables a complicated chemical reaction to reverse the combustion process. Through the nanotechnology-based catalyst containing multiple reaction sites, the solution of CO_2 dissolved in water is turned into ethanol with a yield of 63%.

TECHNOLOGY SUMMARY

COMPANY NAME:

Oak Ridge National Laboratory
(US Department of Energy)

FEEDSTOCK:

Effluent carbon dioxide

COUNTRY OF ORIGIN:

United States

EQUIPMENT TYPE:

Electrochemical process equipment
(Distributed supply chain)

TECHNOLOGY STATUS (2018):

Ongoing research

CO_2, the main waste product GHG of fossil fuel combustion, is the input stream, and the combustion reaction is pushed backward with very high selectivity to produce (and store) a useful fuel (ethanol). A process like this would allow for the consumption of extra electricity when it is available to make and store as ethanol. This could help balance a grid supplied by intermittent renewable sources.

There is ongoing research with funding from the US DOE under the Technology Innovation Program. Peer-reviewed journal articles published on results to date can be found at: https://www.ornl.gov/content/high-selectivity-electrochemical-conversion-co2-ethanol-using-copper-nanoparticlen-doped. Next step is to license the technology and launch a large-scale demonstration project. The technology is still being developed and not yet commercially proven.

According to Organic Waste System (OWS), DRANCO process is a well-known and reliable anaerobic digestion technology. This technology is marketed throughout the world directly by OWS or by means of its exclusive license partners. OWS claims several years of experience and provides a reasonable reference list (mostly EU with a few in the Republic of Korea/Japan)[28] and case study[29] on its website. Figures 89 and 90 show the process flow diagram and aerial view of DRANCO plant in Hengelo, The Netherlands.

---

[27]   Oak Ridge National Laboratory, US Department of Energy.   Nano-spike catalysts convert carbon dioxide directly into ethanol. https://www.ornl.gov/news/nano-spike-catalysts-convert-carbon-dioxide-directly-ethanol.

[28]   Organic Waste Systems, Inc. (OWS). http://www.ows.be/biogas-plants/references/.

[29]   BIoCycle Refor 20. 2012. http://www.biocyclerefor.com/2012/presents_tuesday/McDonald_s.pdf.

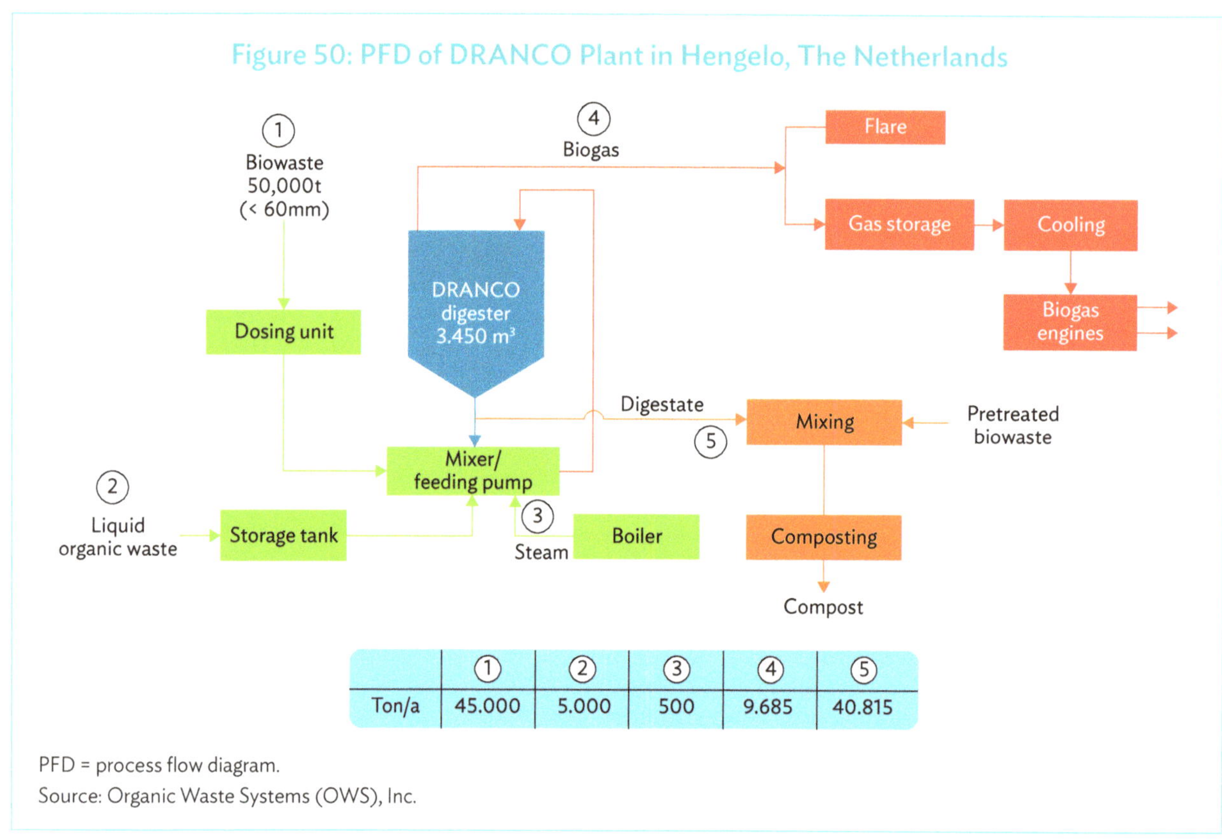

	①	②	③	④	⑤
Ton/a	45.000	5.000	500	9.685	40.815

PFD = process flow diagram.
Source: Organic Waste Systems (OWS), Inc.

Aerial View of DRANCO Plant in Hengelo, The Netherlands. This plant in Hengelo, the Netherlands uses Dry Anaerobic Composting (DRANCO) process, which is an advanced biotechnological process for an environmentally friendly and cost-effective treatment of organics derived from municipal solid waste (photo by Organic Waste Systems, Inc.).

2.9   Sekisui Chemical/LanzaTech

OVERVIEW

Sekisui Chemical Co., Ltd and Lanzatech Inc.[30] developed a technology that transforms waste into ethanol. The combustible waste is gasified and the gas produced is converted into ethanol using a microbial catalyst.

TECHNOLOGY SUMMARY

Municipal and industrial wastes are heterogeneous in nature with varying components and composition. Sekisui Chemical and Lanzatech developed a waste-to-ethanol production method wherein heterogeneous waste, without any sorting, is gasified through an existing technology to break down waste into molecular level (CO, H2) at low-oxygen conditions. Through the gasification process, feedstock attains a simplified and more homogenous characteristics while retaining the energy contents of the source waste.

TECHNOLOGY SUMMARY

COMPANY NAME:

Sekisui Chemical Co., Ltd & LanzaTech, Inc.

FEEDSTOCK:

Municipal solid waste

COUNTRY OF ORIGIN:

Japan

EQUIPMENT TYPE:

Waste to ethanol
(distributed supply chain)

TECHNOLOGY STATUS (2018):

Pilot demonstration

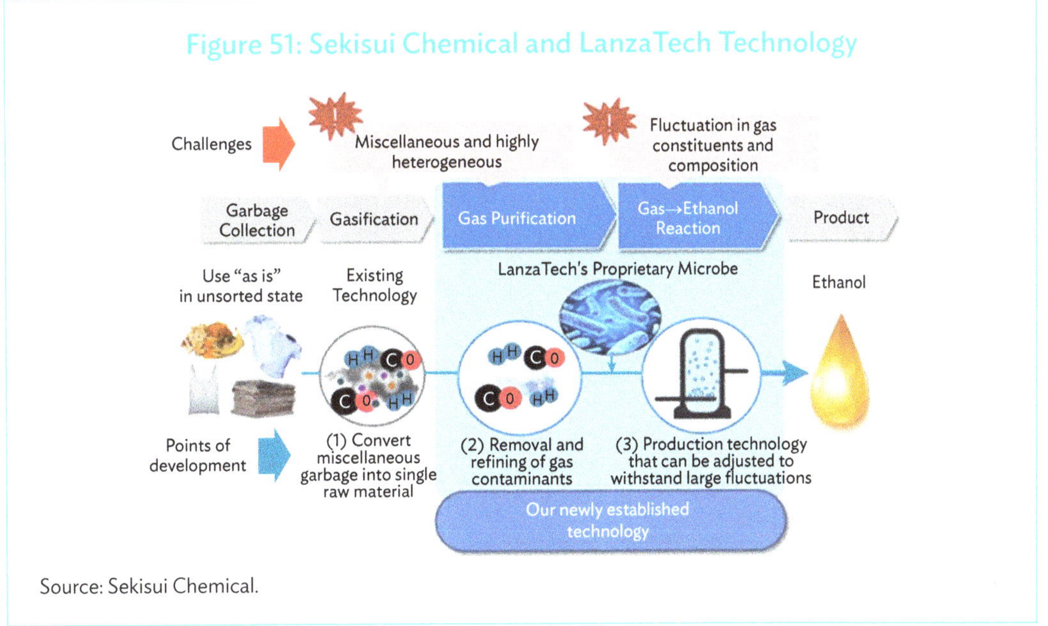

Figure 51: Sekisui Chemical and LanzaTech Technology

Source: Sekisui Chemical.

30   Sekisui Chemical. 2017. *Turning "Garbage" into Ethanol: Establishing a First-in-The-World Innovative Production Technology.* Osaka. https://www.sekisuichemical.com/whatsnew/2017/1325318_29675.html.

However, the gas produced from unsorted waste contains a lot of impurities, which is not compatible with microbial catalysts. Thus, both Sekisui Chemical and Lanzatech developed a two-gas clean-up technology that is compatible to the living microbial catalyst. Microbial catalyst enables the production of ethanol without requiring external input of heat and pressure. Lanzatech's engineered microbes have reaction speed of 10 times that of native microorganisms and can achieve high-speed production to adequately meet industrial levels.

The whole process is completed by establishing a fermentation control technology to adjust fluctuations in feedstock compositions and maintain stability of microbial conditions (Figure 91). The technology can also handle different kinds of risks associated with disposal facilities such as gasifier blockage and gas outages.

In cooperation with ORIX Environmental Resources Management Corporation, Sekisui Chemical constructed a pilot plant within a disposal facility in Yori-machi, Saitama Prefecture, Japan. Of continuous development since 2014, Sekisui Chemical has produced ethanol from collected waste with high production efficiency.

Sekisui Chemical is currently promoting the benefit of the technology to wide range of stakeholders including national administrative bodies in Japan. Sekisui aims to have the first production plant into operation by 2019.[31] Moreover, Sekisui believes that its initiative is in line with the directive of the Cabinet of Japan through its Investments for the Future Strategy 2017 of formulating strategies to achieve a carbon-recycling society through the use of biotechnology. Figure 92 shows Sekisui's ultimate recycling system.

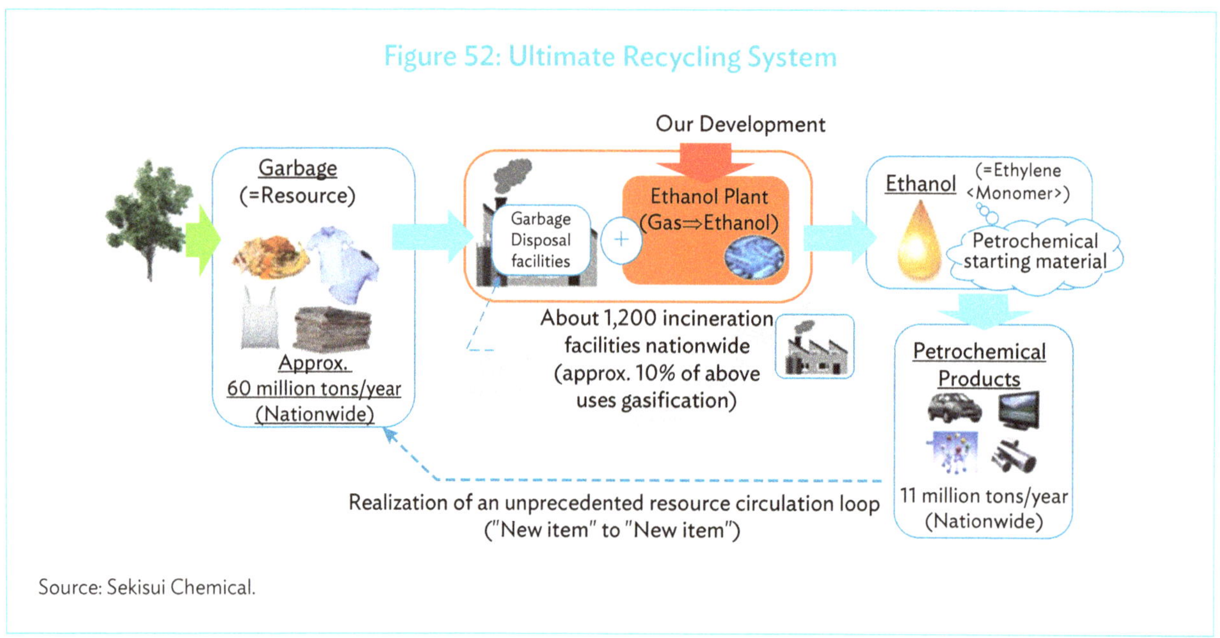

Source: Sekisui Chemical.

---

31   Sekisui Company. 2020. SEKISUI CHEMICAL and Sumitomo Chemical to Cooperate on Circular Economy Initiative Manufacturing Polyolefin using Waste as Raw Material. 27 February. https://www.sekisuichemical.com/whatsnew/2020/1347675_36556.html.

2.10   Walbruze Waste Energy Management

OVERVIEW

Walbruze Waste Energy Management developed an incineration technology through thermochemical processing. The first step is a mechanical sorting and thermal extrusion process that results in output of a uniform burning, and thus more efficient, solid recovered fuel (SRF). In the second step, the SRF is then burned in an incinerator boiler coupled with steam turbine generator to produce electricity.

TECHNOLOGY SUMMARY

The core process generates SRF from the waste by means of a homogenization extruder machine, which comprises of a main body with feed opening, an extruder screw, an outlet, and compression cone.

TECHNOLOGY SUMMARY

COMPANY NAME:

Walbruze Waste Energy Management

FEEDSTOCK:

Solid waste

COUNTRY OF ORIGIN:

Indonesia

EQUIPMENT TYPE:

Thermo-mechanical processing (Distributed supply chain)

TECHNOLOGY STATUS (2018):

Prototype; results unverified

The machine is simple to install and operate. On an average, it reduces waste volume by 80% and increases density by 650% (resulting in saving in handling and storage), while forming homogeneous SRF briquettes. The SRF produced can replace coal or mixed with coal biomass briquette. The equipment and production process of the Wastrong machine is shown in Figure 93.

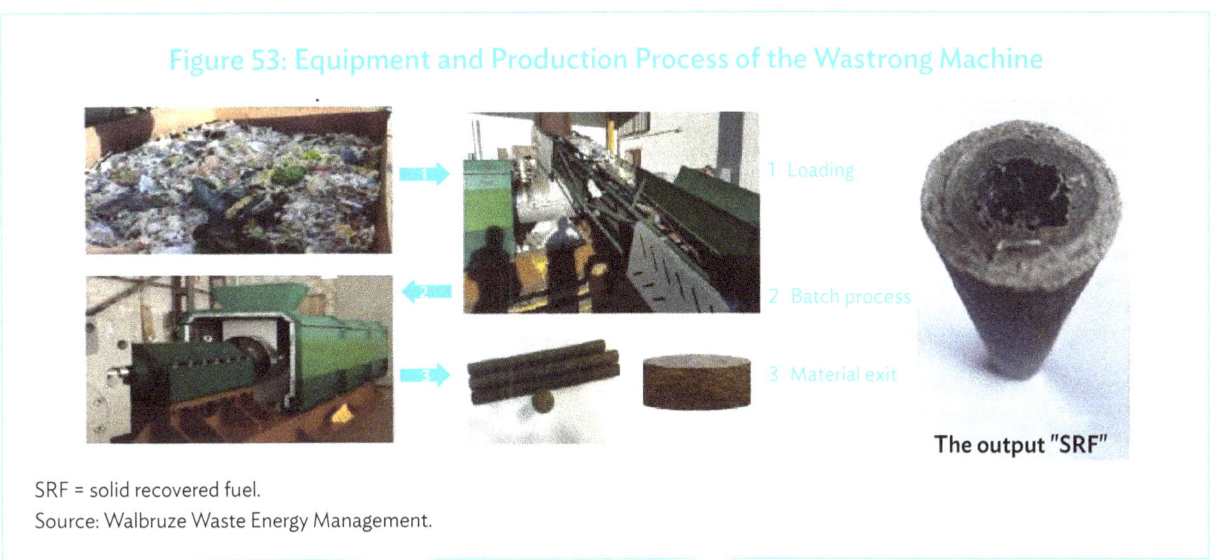

Figure 53: Equipment and Production Process of the Wastrong Machine

SRF = solid recovered fuel.
Source: Walbruze Waste Energy Management.

2.11   Ecalox

OVERVIEW

Ecalox is a startup company. Its technology converts waste low-grade aluminum to hydrogen fuel. A pilot unit amounting to $200,000 could be evaluated and fit well in the circular economy model. This technology is consistent with the known reaction of aluminum with water in the pres ence of gallium catalyst to form hydrogen

$$2Al + 3H_2O \rightarrow 3H_2 + Al_2O_3 + heat$$

TECHNOLOGY SUMMARY

The technology has the potential to use waste aluminum to produce three valuable outputs with zero carbon emission: hydrogen that can be used as fuel, aloxites that can be sold in the market, and harnessable process heat.

Projected business model:

(i)   A ton of delivered low-grade small-particle aluminum waste costs around $400. Long-term multiyear contracts are available for this material.

(ii)   Every ton of aluminum processed generates 103 kilograms of high-purity hydrogen worth $500–$900 at current prices.

(iii) Every ton of aluminum converted to hydrogen also generates process heat of 4.5 megawatt thermal (MWt)—a figure based on published research by the US DOE and Ecalox data. The UK Department for Business, Energy and Industrial Strategy (www.DECC.gov.uk) figures value this at $700.

(iv)   Every ton of aluminum processed generates 1.8 tons of clean white zero-carbon aloxites worth $1000.

Based on the above, not considering depreciation and OPEX, $400 of raw material results in $2,200–$2,600 of product with zero carbon footprint.

Also, every ton of aluminum processed generates 0.01% (estimated) of the CO_2 emission of the most efficient known electrolysis or steam methane reforming system. This figure is based on Ecalox's data of 1 kWh start-up energy for every 100 kWh produced.

Overall if the results can be corroborated, this is an extremely useful technology.

REFERENCES

Biofuels Digest. 2015. United Airlines Invests $30M in Fulcrum BioEnergy; Inks $1.5B+ in Aviation Biofuels Contracts. https://www.biofuelsdigest.com/bdigest/2015/06/30/united-airlines-invests-30m-in-fulcrum-bioenergy-inks-1-5b-in-aviation-biofuels-contracts/. Also appeared in Insidewaste. 2015. https://www.insidewaste.com.au/general/news/1002437/united-airlines-invests-usd30m-msw-biofuel.

BloCycle Refor 20. 2012. http://www.biocyclerefor.com/2012/presents_tuesday/McDonald_s.pdf.

Cogent Energy Systems. www.cogentenergysystems.com.

EcoFuel Technologies. Renewables and Environment. Michigan. www.ecofueltechnology.com.

Ecoprog GmbH. 2019. *Waste to Energy 2019/2020: Technologies, Plants, Projects, Players and Backgrounds of the Global Thermal Waste Treatment Business*. Extract. 12th ed. Cologne. https://www.ecoprog.com/fileadmin/user_upload/extract_market_report_WtE_2019-2020_ecoprog.pdf.

Enerkem. *Setting a New Sustainable Standard in Waste Management around the World*. https://enerkem.com.

Enerkem. *Waste Management World*. https://waste-management-world.com/tag/Enerkem.

Fulcrum BioEnergy. fulcrum-bioenergy.com.

Government of Canada. 2018. Technology Readiness Levels. 23 January. https://www.ic.gc.ca/eic/site/080.nsf/eng/00002.html - technology readiness levels.

Government of Thailand, Ministry of Energy. 2015. Alternative Energy Development Plan: AEDP2015. Department of Renewable Energy Development and Energy Efficiency. September.

ideas*. Melbourne. www.ideaservices.com.au.

InEnTec. *Clean Planet Technologies*. Richland, WA. www.inentec.com.

J. Doherty. 2019. 'Mechanical Challenges' Delay Ørsted Bioliquid Plant. *Environment Media Group*. 31 January. https://www.letsrecycle.com/news/latest-news/mechanical-challenges-delay-orsted-bioliquid-plant/.

Orsted. https://orsted.com/en/About-us.

Oak Ridge National Laboratory, US Department of Energy. Nano-spike catalysts convert carbon dioxide directly into ethanol. https://www.ornl.gov/news/nano-spike-catalysts-convert-carbon-dioxide-directly-ethanol.

Organic Waste Systems, Inc. (OWS). http://www.ows.be/biogas-plants/references/.

P. Kong. Cogent Energy Systems. Federal Laboratory Consortium for Technology Transfer. 2020. https://federallabs.org/successes/awards/awards-gallery/2019/cogent-energy-systems.

Paritta Wangkiat. 2018. Policy May Well Energise Alternative Power. *Bangkok Post*. 5 April. https://www. bangkokpost.com/opinion/opinion/1440954/policy-may-well-energise-alternative-power.

Pragmatec. *Pyro-Kat Environmental Technologies*. Vienna. www.pragmatec.at/en/pyro-kat-environmental-technology.

SAFE s.pa. http://www.safegas.it/en/.

Sekisui Chemical. 2017. *Turning "Garbage" into Ethanol: Establishing a First-in-The-World Innovative Production Technology*. Osaka. https://www.sekisuichemical.com/whatsnew/2017/1325318_29675.html.

Sekisui Company. 2020. SEKISUI CHEMICAL and Sumitomo Chemical to Cooperate on Circular Economy Initiative Manufacturing Polyolefin using Waste as Raw Material. 27 February. https://www.sekisuichemical. com/whatsnew/2020/1347675_36556.html.

Waste Management World. 2017. *In-Depth: Ionic Gasifier Opens Up Door to Small-Scale Waste-to-Energy*. July. https://waste-management-world.com/a/in-depth-ionic-gasifier-opens-up-door-to-small-scale-waste-to-energy.